Lunch at the 5 & 10

The Four. Left to right: David Richmond, Franklin McCain, Ezell Blair Jr., Joseph McNeil. *Photo: Jack Moebes, Greensboro Record.*

Lunch at the 5 & 10

MILES WOLFF

REVISED AND EXPANDED EDITION

INTRODUCTION BY AUGUST MEIER

Elephant Paperbacks
Ivan R. Dee, Publisher, Chicago

To my father—
a newspaperman

LUNCH AT THE 5 & 10. Copyright © 1970, 1990 by Miles Wolff.
Introduction copyright © 1990 by August Meier. All rights reserved,
including the right to reproduce this book or portions thereof in
any form. For information, address: Ivan R. Dee, Inc., 1332 North
Halsted Street, Chicago 60622. Manufactured in the United States
of America and printed on acid-free paper.

Library of Congress Cataloging-in-Publication Data:
Wolff, Miles.
    Lunch at the 5 & 10 / Miles Wolff ; intro. by August Meier—Rev. ed.
    p.   cm.
    Rev. ed. of: Lunch at the five and ten. 1970.
    Includes index.
    Summary: A detailed account of the sit-in at a Woolworth's lunch coun-
ter in Greensboro, North Carolina, in 1960, which ignited the civil rights
movement in the United States.
    ISBN 0-929587-31-6 (alk. paper)
    1. Afro-Americans—North Carolina—Greensboro. 2. Afro-Americans—
North Carolina—Greensboro—Civil rights. 3. Civil rights demonstrations—
North Carolina—Greensboro. 4. Greensboro (N.C.)—Race relations.
[1. Civil rights demonstrations. 2. Afro-Americans—History—1877–1964.
3. Greensboro (N.C.)—Race relations.] I. Wolff, Miles. Lunch at
the five and ten. II. Title. III. Title: Lunch at the 5 and 10.
IV. Title: Lunch at the five & ten.
F264.G8W6   1990
975.6'62—dc20   90-32620

Contents

Preface to the 1990 Edition

IN DISCUSSING a new edition of this book, one of the issues was whether to change some of the language. Specifically, how were we to refer to black Americans? Most of the work for this study was done in 1966, and the word "Negro" was then used more often, though "colored" was still accepted. When the book was published in 1970, the change in usage to "black" was taking place, and my editor wondered whether we should change the references accordingly. But because the change was starting and still not totally accepted, we stayed with "Negro."

Now, in 1990, the question again arises, but now it is whether to stay with "Negro," go to "black," or change to what seems to be a new direction and use "African American." Again, the decision has been made to stay with the original version. Chiefly the reason is to try to give a feel for the mood of 1960 and to use the language of the period.

In rereading the book, I note other phrases that might have been changed. I refer to the four A & T freshmen as "boys," when now the usage would be "students" or "young men." Other descriptions might now be left out.

3

But I hope there is value in leaving the work as it was originally written, and that the reader will know this comes from an era when many of the changes that have occurred in race relations were just beginning.

M. W.

Durham, North Carolina
March 1990

Introduction

1990, WHICH marks the thirtieth anniversary of the black college student sit-ins that swept the South in the spring of 1960, is a most appropriate time to reissue Miles Wolff's *Lunch at the 5 & 10*. For this wave of black protest, which began at Greensboro, North Carolina, on February 1, 1960, marked a decisive turning point in the long history of the African-American struggle for freedom—the beginning of a series of dramatic developments that has in many ways transformed race relations and the status of black Americans in American society.

Negro protest had historically taken the form of appealing to the conscience of white Americans, by reminding them of the country's fundamental democratic values, and seeking remedies through legislation and litigation in the courts. In the twentieth century the pre-eminent organization employing this strategy of agitation, lobbying, and litigation has been the National Association for the Advancement of Colored People (NAACP), founded in 1909—during the worst period in the experience of black Americans since the Civil War—by a small group of prominent black intellectuals and white liberals. The NAACP within a decade became firmly established in the black community under the dynamic leadership of a black executive and field staff. Its most important contribution was its litigation to secure fulfillment of the 14th and 15th Amendments, including campaigns against mob violence; against segregation in publicly owned facilities and places of public accommodation; against disfranchisement in the Southern states; and against segregation in the public schools. By the latter part of the 1950s, in fact, much had been achieved in the way of court victories, though in practice these Supreme Court decisions were largely violated, especially in the Deep South.

Occasionally, also, blacks had used other tactics—boycotts, picketing, mass marches, and sit-ins—which collectively are now known as forms of direct action. These had been employed spontaneously in black communities from time to time, most notably in the recurring use of the boycott to fight school segregation in the North, the use of the same tactics in the South to protest the inauguration of streetcar segregation early in this century, and the widespread "Don't Buy Where You Can't Work" campaigns during the 1930s. It was not until 1942, with the founding of the Congress of Racial Equality (CORE), that conscious use of direct-action techniques, informed by Gandhian nonviolent theory, was proposed as a long-range strategy. CORE pioneered in and perfected the technique of the sit-in as a weapon against discriminatory places of public accommodation and recreation in the North and in St. Louis, and more tentatively against transportation segregation in the Upper South states of Virginia and North Carolina. Then came the boycotts against jim crow local bus transportation in 1954 and 1955 in Baton Rouge and Montgomery, the latter propelling to fame Martin Luther King, Jr., who adopted as his philosophy the pacifist ideology of Mahatma Gandhi. And during the 1950s, especially toward the end of the decade, NAACP youth councils and college students in border cities from Oklahoma City to Baltimore were staging successful sit-ins.

In retrospect, what happened in 1960 thus appears to have been a logical next step. This was especially so because the NAACP victories before the Supreme Court, the events in Montgomery, and the attainment of independence by African colonies beginning with Ghana in 1957 had changed the perspective of American blacks, inducing greater militancy and what has widely been called a "revolution in expectations." Court decisions and legislation had brought changes only so far. Something more militant seemed called for in order to fulfill the promise engendered by NAACP victories and to hasten the pace of social change. Not surprisingly, such sentiments were strongest among the younger generation. Students at institutions other than North Carolina A & T (and especially college youth in Nashville) were thinking of adopting nonviolent direct tactics, and what seemed at the time to be the totally spontaneous action of the four black youth in Greensboro met an enthusiastic response among black youth across the South, thus inaugurating an unprecedented period of black activism and social change.

Miles Wolff chronicled in depth the sit-in campaign against exclusionary variety-store lunch counters in Greensboro from its start in February until the stores capitulated in June, and until victory was attained on July 25. It is not surprising that these college student sit-ins started in an Upper South city like Greensboro, for in retrospect the Upper South cities were the next probable place for sit-ins to occur, once some success had been achieved in border cities. Wolff gives us an account based on talks with both the black actors in this drama and the whites who became involved in responding to the students' challenge. One of the virtues of his narrative is that it supplies us with a dose of historical realism: it compels us to revise the mythology that arose at the time about the four young men's completely autonomous spontaneity. The role of a white merchant (with a store in Greensboro's black community) in encouraging their action was known only to very few at the time. This is a highly ironic fact, because the positive response of these particular youth to his suggestion of sitting-in at the variety stores was rooted in the growing militancy of college students across the South. In fact, if the student sit-in movement had not been inaugurated in Greensboro that day, it would surely have been ignited elsewhere (most probably in Nashville, another Upper South city where, as in Greensboro, blacks enjoyed the franchise).

Following the first sit-in in Greensboro, students organized themselves in dramatic fashion for demonstrations in city after city, not only across the Upper South but also in the Deep South, where they were universally crushed by the coercive power of law enforcement agencies and even by outright violence from intransigent whites. Thousands were arrested, but during the following months in a number of cities, almost entirely in the Upper South and in parts of Florida and Texas, variety stores desegregated their lunch counters.

The sit-ins inaugurated a series of momentous developments. The victories achieved through this student activism (modest though they now seem in retrospect) brought a decisive break with the pre-eminence of the NAACP's legal tactics (vital though these remained); stimulated the revival of CORE; led to the forming of a new organization—

8

the Student Nonviolent Coordinating Committee (SNCC); and ushered in a period of spirited rivalry—and greatly increased activity—among these and other racial advancement organizations: the NAACP, the National Urban League, and Dr. King's Southern Christian Leadership Conference. Direct-action tactics were renewed in the North, against segregated schools, exclusionary housing practices, and employment discrimination. In 1963 another massive wave of direct action swept over the South, involving all sectors of the black community and epitomized by the campaign in Birmingham led by Martin Luther King. Meanwhile, with philanthropic funding, voter registration efforts were mounted across the South—again, however, meeting sharp resistance (including violence) in Deep Southern communities, where the danger to those attempting to register was so serious, and the whites so stubborn, that voter registration itself functioned as a form of direct action. All these developments culminated in the passage of the Civil Rights Acts of 1964 and 1965, whose provisions overthrew segregation in public accommodations, pretty well undermined black disfranchisement, and did much to further the cause of equal opportunity in employment. Ironically, while direct-action tactics effectively mobilized a changing white public opinion to support racial reform by dramatizing as they did the evils of racist practices, their most substantial victory in the end was the new civil rights laws whose tortuous course through Congress was managed under the leadership of the NAACP.

By the time the law of 1965 was passed, direct-action demonstrations had waned and virtually disappeared. But they had accomplished much, so much in fact that they produced a new revolution in expectations and new demands on society to rectify black grievances—demands

9

which, along with the many changes in the Negro's status, remain with us today as the legacy of the student protest of 1960. Thus the turning point inaugurated by the Greensboro Four produced continuing ramifications to the present day.

AUGUST MEIER

Kent State University
April 1990

1

The First Day

What's going on down there?
Nothing!

AT FOUR-THIRTY the four boys sat down at the lunch counter. They were Negroes, students at North Carolina Agricultural and Technical College (A & T), a state Negro college located in Greensboro. It was not the first time that Negroes had sat at a Woolworth's lunch counter, nor the first time A & T students had asked for service, and the reaction would be the same as in any white eating establishment in the South in 1960: "We don't serve colored here." The boys were not newcomers ignorant of local customs, and they knew Woolworth's served Negroes only at the stand-up snack bar, but they took seats on the stools at the counter and waited for their orders to be taken.

The four had entered the store a little earlier. Two of them had bought toothpaste, combs, and other small articles in the toiletries area, and they brought these items and their receipts with them to the lunch counter. On the counter, a small stand advertised a turkey club sandwich at sixty-five cents. As the waitress approached, Ezell Blair Jr., the smallest of the group, spoke: "I'd like a cup of coffee, please." The waitress answered as expected: "I'm sorry. We don't serve Negroes here." But the four did not leave, and the boy said: "I beg to disagree with you. You just finished serving me at a counter only two feet away from here." The waitress pointed to the stand-up counter and said, "Negroes eat at the other end."

The boy went on. "What do you mean? This is a public place, isn't it? If it isn't, then why don't you sell membership cards? If you do that, then I'll understand that this is a private concern." The waitress responded a little more heatedly, "Well, you won't get any service here!" and walked away. The boys remained in their seats, and a Negro girl, a helper on the steam table, approached them and told the four that Negroes were not served at the lunch counter. When they did not move, she became angry. "You're acting stupid, ignorant! That's why we can't get anywhere today. You know you're supposed to eat at the other end." The boys stayed seated.

The date was February 1, 1960, and the four boys were starting a sit-in. There had been earlier demonstrations at variety stores and earlier sit-ins. One of the early movements of the Congress of Racial Equality (CORE) had been against segregated eating facilities of Woolworth's in Baltimore. And in Wichita, Kansas, and in Oklahoma City, Oklahoma, in 1958, there had been a partially successful lunch-counter protest, with more than thirty restaurants opening their doors as a result. In Greensboro there had been a sit-in when Jackie Robinson, catching a plane out of the city, refused to go to the Negro waiting room and continued sitting in the white section of the terminal. But these protests had stopped where they started, and throughout the South the pattern of segregated facilities remained.

The aim of the students was purely local: to obtain service in a store which welcomed Negroes at all but one counter. But these particular four Negro students, sitting at a Woolworth's lunch counter dressed in coats and ties, were starting something that was not to stop with one lunch counter.

The Woolworth's store in Greensboro is probably not much different from any other Woolworth's store in the nation. It has the familiar red sign with gold lettering announcing "F. W. Woolworth," and inside are the long parallel counters arranged with merchandise. On the north and west sides of the store is an L-shaped lunch counter which in 1960 could seat sixty-six. It is a fairly large store, taking up three floors—a basement, a main floor, and a second floor used for storage and offices—and the store is on Greensboro's second busiest corner. It is located on South Elm Street in the heart of the city, one block from the intersection of Elm and Market Streets, the intersection the Chamber of Commerce proudly calls the "Crossroads of the Carolinas."

For the downtown Greensboro Woolworth's, the lunch counter is the largest single money-maker. The Greensboro downtown is deteriorating, and there are few places to eat, and Woolworth's is a convenient and fairly inexpensive place to eat. The food is adequate, and the store's bakery, which makes its own cakes and pastries, is one of the better bakeries in the city.

In 1960 the store was managed by C. L. Harris, a balding man known as "Curly," a man proud of his store and proud of Woolworth's. In his gray suit, he looked the part of a Woolworth's manager, and it was a role he liked. His office was on the second floor, but he was rarely in it. Usually he could be found on the main floor, checking displays, arranging goods, talking to customers, or sitting at the

13

C. L. Harris, Manager of Woolworth's at the time of the sit-ins.
Photo: *Greensboro Daily News.*

lunch counter, checking over figures or just talking over a cup of coffee. Harris had money of his own and no longer needed to work, but he liked the job, and he liked retailing. He started with the company in 1923, working his way (at Woolworth's) through Duke University, and although he studied to be a certified public accountant, and worked for a time as one, he always came back to Woolworth's. As he put it, "Retailing is in my blood."

Harris disliked the store's being called a "five and ten" or a "dime store"; he preferred the title "junior department store" or at least "variety store." He liked to point out the

14

$150 television sets, forty-dollar watches, and other expensive items to prove his point. When he started, F. W. Woolworth & Co. was strictly a five and ten, and he liked to say that he was in the first store in the Southeast district that sold items costing more than a dime. He worked over the years to raise the prestige of Woolworth's, doing this by increasing the quality and type of merchandise.

On the afternoon of February 1, C. L. Harris was upstairs in his second-floor office when one of the waitresses came in to tell him that there were four colored boys at the lunch counter who would not move. Harris immediately told her, "Let them sit there. Don't say anything else to them." Two or three years earlier he had anticipated this problem and had written to the regional office in Atlanta asking what to do if Negroes refused to leave when asked. In the letter he had suggested that Woolworth's should just let them sit, under the assumption that if the store ignored them, the Negroes would become bored and leave. The regional office recommended that his suggestion be followed if the problem ever arose. The company did not want to arrest any customers.

Nonetheless, Harris was worried, and he immediately started for the police station, three blocks away. As might be expected, the store manager remembers the day well. Outside it was sunny and warm, and he recalls not needing a topcoat—unusual for the first of February.

Inside the store the boys continued to sit: Ezell Blair Jr., Franklin McCain, Joseph McNeil, and David Richmond. Blair and Richmond were from Greensboro, McNeil from Wilmington, North Carolina, and McCain, who had lived in Greensboro most of his life, now made his home in Washington, D.C. They had not come to Woolworth's

15

on the spur of the moment; they were fully aware of what they were doing and fully expecting to be arrested. In fact, bond was waiting for them.

The four were freshmen at A & T, eighteen years old, and like many freshmen, they had dreams and plans. They were idealistic and perhaps a little naïve. The four boys had been discussing the idea of asking for service at Woolworth's for almost a month. Joe McNeil had brought it up in a bull session, and as McCain put it, "McNeil had an idea we should do something different from most people and I decided I could be as big a fool as he could." Then on the night of January 31, McNeil came into his room where the other three were talking and asked if they were ready to go. At first the others thought he was kidding, but then Franklin McCain, the largest of the four, spoke up: "Are you guys chicken or not?" The answer, of course, was No.

As the four sat at the counter, they were scared ("Sure we were scared. I suppose if anyone had come up behind me and yelled 'Boo' I think I would have fallen off my seat."), but as they continued sitting and no one else came up to tell them to go and no policeman came in to arrest them, an idea hit McCain. "We didn't know what they could do to us, we didn't know how long we could sit. Now it came to me all of a sudden: Maybe they can't do anything to us. Maybe we can keep it up."

Harris was in the police station to see just how long they could keep it up. He had gone directly to the chief of police, Paul Calhoun, but Calhoun told him the police could not interfere unless the store wished to issue a trespass warrant. Harris replied that he did not want to serve them with a warrant, he just wanted them away from his lunch counter. Harris remembers that Calhoun was not

16

overly concerned, and the chief said it would "probably blow over." He did, however, send a couple of officers to the store to make certain no trouble developed. Harris remained with the police chief until 5:15.

At 5:00, Jo Spivey of the Greensboro evening *Record* received a call that there was a story up at Woolworth's. She knew the caller, but he said he would rather his name didn't get mixed up in the story. She was at home at the time, but called the newspaper office for a photographer to go to the store and see what was happening.

A few minutes later, Dr. George Simkins, a Negro dentist and head of the Greensboro chapter of the National Association for the Advancement of Colored People, also received a call. "Well, I've done it!" Simkins heard as he picked up the phone. He knew the caller but did not have the slightest idea what the man was talking about. "You've done what?" Simkins asked, and was told about the four boys. Five months earlier the same man had tried to get Simkins to sit in at Woolworth's, but the dentist quite frankly doubted that attempting to get service at a variety store would accomplish anything, and he was involved in a court case over desegregation of a public golf course, which was taking up most of his time. But now that the four boys were at Woolworth's, he promised to do anything he could to help.

On East Market Street, Dorothy Graves walked toward Woolworth's. A Negro employee at a small clothing store on the same street, she had told her employer that they were out of thread and she was going to Woolworth's to get some. Both she and her boss knew that the real reason she was going to Woolworth's was to see what had happened to four boys who had left the store a few minutes earlier.

17

As Harris made his way back to the store, he met *Record* photographer Jack Moebes, also on the way to Woolworth's. Moebes greeted Harris with "What's going on down there?" and Harris said, "Nothing!" Moebes walked along with Harris, saying he knew there was a story because a note had been left on the city desk. He was going to find out. "No one is going to take any pictures in my store," said Harris.

There is some dispute over what time the two men reached the store. Harris says it was 5:30, the store's normal closing time, while other reports have it that the store closed fifteen minutes early. Whatever time it was, Moebes was not allowed to come in the store, as the front doors were locked and the store closed.

The boys were still sitting. Two policemen had come into the store and walked behind the four, but nothing was said. Outside a small crowd was gathering and a photographer waiting, and with the doors locked, Ezell Blair Jr. went over to a public phone and made a call. "Number One, this is Number Three. They've closed the doors. What should we do?" "Keep sitting," was the reply. Blair returned to the counter.

Harris believes that some organization or some person other than the four boys was involved in starting the sit-ins. He does not know about the telephone call Blair made nor the call Dr. Simkins received, but he does know about the presence of the newspaper photographer, the gathering crowd, and the general actions of the students in the store that suggested some planning. Harris is correct.

The A & T campus is located off East Market Street about a mile and a half from the center of Greensboro. It presents a modern face to the observer, for most of its buildings have been built within the past ten or fifteen years, partly as a result of Supreme Court decisions which prompted Southern legislators to improve Negro schools and colleges. It is the largest Negro college in the state—there are over three thousand students, male and female—and it is located in what is considered the Negro section of Greensboro. The four boys met in the library that Monday, February 1, and then started walking along East Market Street toward town. But they did not go immediately to Woolworth's; at 3 P.M. they entered a small clothing store in the 200 block of East Market Street. They went directly to the back of the store.

Jack Dempsey, Joe Louis, Max Schmeling, Gene Tunney, Jim Braddock, Max Baer—fighters in the golden age of boxing, when the glamour of the fight game was at its peak—heavyweight champions of the world. This was the time of million-dollar gates, an era when the heavyweight championship fight could make people forget the soaring stock market of the twenties or the lengthening bread lines of the thirties, a time in which to be near the champ was to be near fame. From Yankee Stadium, Soldiers Field, Philadelphia's Municipal Stadium, or wherever heavyweight championships were fought, newspapers sent hundreds of reporters to cover the big fight, to send back thousands of words of copy.

Photographers were there also, and in newspapers across the country, pictures were carried of the victorious heavyweight champion surrounded by trainers, officials, and newspapermen. And out of these photographs from a now dead era of the champ being surrounded by crowds in the rings, the face of a dark-eyed teenager looks out. Sometimes he is in the back of the crowd surrounding the champ, sometimes he is reaching over to touch him, and sometimes

19

he is raising the victorious hand of the heavyweight champion of the world. If there is a photograph of the knockout victim, this same intense youth is often seen dragging the victim to his corner.

He is neither reporter, trainer, nor official—he is not connected with the fight game—and the heavyweight champions whose hands he raises are undoubtedly unaware of who he is. But this is a young man with a purpose, striving toward a goal he has sought since he was twelve years old.

As his pictures continue to appear in photos of heavyweight fights, sports editors around the country pick up his story. They begin to term him the new "One-Eyed Connelly," and in Pittsburgh, Al Abrams, sports editor of the *Post Gazette*, terms him the "world's greatest gate crasher." The young man has arrived. Ever since he crashed his first event when he was twelve, he has wanted that title, and by 1935 after six Rose Bowl games, the 1932 Olympics, and every heavyweight championship from Dempsey-Tunney, the young gate crasher has achieved his goal. He has hitch-hiked, ridden the rails, bummed rides on airplanes to get to these events, and at twenty he has been through the forty-eight states, Mexico, and Canada.

The young gate crasher is far from publicity-shy, and at news offices and sports desks around the country, he tells his story. He calls himself "Ruffles" Johns, taking his clippings wherever he goes. He sends letters to the nation's sports writers to let them know of his latest exploits. One writer terms him the "loquacious imitator of One-Eyed Connelly." Before fights he boasts that he will crash the gate, and as he becomes more famous ushers are alerted, but he is always in the ring after a fight, making sure his picture is taken. That is his proof, he tells newspaper reporters.

20

"World's Greatest Gate Crasher" (far left) in the ring with Babe Risko
after Risko won the middleweight championship. *Photo:* Ralph Johns.

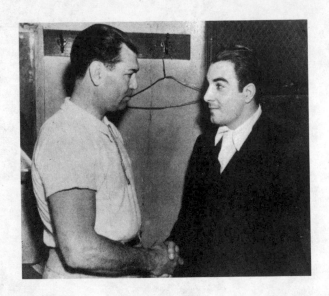

Ralph Johns: with Jack Dempsey, and with Jackie Robinson at an
exhibition game in Greensboro. *Photo:* Ralph Johns.

He has no magic way to crash big events—he just improvises. For the Louis-Schmeling fight, he sleeps under the ring the night before the fight, and for another big fight he spends the night in Yankee Stadium. He admits to defeat only once, and that is for a middleweight fight in California where the local police handcuffed him to a fence outside the arena. He boasts, "I have carried more heavyweight champions to their corners than any man alive."

When the four walked into the clothing store that Monday before going to Woolworth's, they immediately went to the owner, Ralph Johns. The name of the store was simply "Ralph Johns," and it was a small clothing store, entirely on one floor with only Johns and one part-time assistant to wait on customers. There was not much to distinguish it from any other small clothing store with relatively cheap merchandise, except that on the walls were large blown-up photographs of the owner with Joe Louis, Eleanor Roosevelt, Al Jolson, and others. There were even pictures of him with Abbott and Costello, and one of him dressed in sheik's garb as Rudolph Valentino.

When Johns saw the four, he knew why they were there. "Well, I thought I'd never see you again," he said to McNeil, and McNeil answered, "I told you I'd be back." Immediately Johns took the four to the rear of the store and began coaching them on what to say and how to act when they arrived at Woolworth's. The boys rehearsed for some time; Johns gave them money to buy toothpaste and other articles, and told them to be sure and keep their receipts. He had bond money ready for use when they were arrested, and he was set to call the newspapers. Johns himself wanted no publicity, and he made the boys promise not to reveal his name. A system was arranged whereby no

23

names would be used. Johns became Number One; McNeil, Number Two; Blair, Number Three; McCain, Number Four; and Richmond, Number Five. At about 4:00, the boys left the store.

The road from the "world's greatest gate crasher" to the back of a small, run-down clothing store was not what the young man bent on fame and glory would have desired, and for Ralph Johns the dreams of youth were not the reality of 1960. It was 1936 when the twenty-year-old "Ruffles" Johns announced to the press that he was going to attempt the biggest gate crash of his young career. He was going to stowaway to Europe, crash the Olympics in Germany, and then go on around the world on five dollars that boxing promoter Mike Jacobs had given him.

On the Cunard–White Star Line's *Laconia,* a young third-class passenger was having considerable luck at the shipboard games. In a horseracing game, he had increased a five-dollar beginning to over $150. Unfortunately he signed a receipt for the money using his own name, and the ungracious loser checked the name on the receipt against the list of passengers. "Ruffles" Johns was arrested by the ship's captain as a stowaway, and when the ship arrived in England he was refused the right to land and was sent back to the United States on the next departing liner.

Johns's gate-crashing days were over. No longer interested in that life, he started looking for something else. He was the son of Syrian immigrants, and his father had worked in the steel mills around New Castle, Pennsylvania, ever since coming to the United States at the age of fourteen. But for the second son in a family of nine, the steel mills had little attraction. He attended Duquesne University for a short time, but for a twenty-one-year-old with a de-

24

sire for fame, glory, and publicity, there was only one place to go. In 1937, he left for Hollywood.

It was not as easy to crash Hollywood as to crash the big fights, and for the first few years Johns worked mainly as a stand-in or in bit parts, usually as a heavy in gangster films. In 1939 the swarthy Syrian's big chance came in the form of a screen test for the part of Rudolph Valentino in *The Life of Valentino*. But the role never came through, and a discouraged Johns came East. In 1940 he joined the Army Air Corps.

Johns had picked up some knowledge of Spanish in his travels in the Southwest and Mexico when he was a teen-ager, bumming across the country, and the Army in a rare stroke of logic assigned him to the Caribbean. During this period he wrote a song called *Rock-a-Bye Moon* which was published, but for the most part his war years proved uneventful.

In 1944 Johns was discharged from the Army's Over-seas Replacement Depot (ORD), which was located in Greensboro. He married a local girl and remained in the town. His father-in-law, who was in the clothing business, set him up in a store on East Market Street, and because of its nearness to the Negro section of town it began to cater mainly to Negroes. Around the city Johns soon became known as a nut or simply a nigger-lover. He became a member of the NAACP in the late forties and was very active in helping the students at A & T and Bennett, a local Negro Methodist college for girls. He propped a slate sign outside his store on the sidewalk to advertise the specials for the day but gradually this came to be an editorial voice for Johns. He would write in chalk, "Special for today: Faith, Hope, and Charity," or "God hates Segregation," or "Colored and White fountains are not the way

25

of God or of Christians." Sometimes he simply wrote, "Love thy neighbor." The City Council soon outlawed his outdoor sign for obstructing the sidewalk.

In 1949, Johns approached a student and asked him to test segregation at Woolworth's. He told the student he believed it was unjust for the store to refuse Negroes service at one counter while serving them at another, and he wanted to do something about it. The student he talked to, a football player, said, "Man, what do you want to do? Get me arrested? All I want to do is get my diploma and get out of the South." Throughout the next ten years he continued to ask students and others to sit in at Woolworth's, but their reactions were similar.

Over the years Johns prospered. He had a large Negro trade and was able to build a home in the fashionable Starmount section of Greensboro. Of course, there were the unpleasant incidents—the beating in the Gridiron Grill by six men, phone calls late at night, obscene letters, bomb threats, and ostracism by the white community—and to Johns, a sensitive person, these things hurt. But he was popular with the Negroes; he greeted his customers as "Cuzzin" and wrote a column entitled "Buzzin' with Cuzzin" in the local Negro newspaper. He was not always what Greensboro would term a good businessman. He was a sucker for any hard-luck story, and on his books at one point had notations for over two hundred thousand dollars in loans, bad checks, and credit he was never able to collect.

In December 1959, Joe McNeil came into his store. Johns was fond of talking civil rights with the A & T students (many of them thought he was too liberal on this matter), and on this day he started talking to McNeil, a student he had known for some time. Not surprisingly, he

26

talked about Woolworth's and the hypocrisy of their cheerfully taking Negroes' money at every counter but the lunch counter. He asked McNeil, as he had been asking students for ten years, to try to get service at the lunch counter.

Johns honestly believed he could get the local Woolworth's to integrate if only some students with courage would test the counter. He knew they might get themselves arrested, but he felt that sitting in would put the situation before the community's eyes. Local pressure would force the variety store to integrate.

Johns told McNeil he would coach him in the things to say and would supply bail and any legal fees that might result from the action. McNeil agreed to the plan. When he left, Johns talked about it with Dorothy Graves, his employee since the early fifties. "Just like the rest?" he asked her. "Yeah. He ain't comin' back."

A month later Johns had neither seen nor heard from McNeil, and he thought his evaluation of McNeil was correct. But if this was indeed the case, an incident that occurred in January had changed McNeil's mind. Returning to school on a bus from New York, he was unable to get service in the lunch room of the Greensboro bus station. On January 31 he met with Blair, McCain, and Richmond. The next day they entered Ralph Johns's store.

There is little in Johns's early background to suggest his interest in civil rights. His parents were working hard to try and support the family, and a steel town like New Castle, Pennsylvania, is not the sort of place where one would be especially aware of the problems of Negroes. But Johns does remember certain incidents in his early travels that made him aware of the situation in the South. He was in El Paso, talking to a group of Mexicans, when authorities

27

threatened to throw him across the border. He was allowed to stay only after he convinced them that he was an American. In Mobile, Alabama, he was riding into town in a freight car with a Negro hobo when a crowd of whites jumped him and savagely beat him for being with the Negro. Once, when he was thumbing through Georgia, he stopped to talk with a Negro on a chain gang outside Savannah. The guard threatened to shoot him if he didn't move to the other side of the road. Johns is also a religious man, and he paraphrases scripture to explain his motivation: "How can you love God if you don't love your brother?" He is an open, frank man who will entreat a friend or a passerby to live like a Christian. He says he tries to live by the single word "love."

But the real reason for Johns's involvement with the Negro lies probably not in any experiences or beliefs, but in his maverick personality. For Johns, a man who dreamed of glory and fame and achieved but little, being banished to a small clothing shop was undoubtedly difficult. He did not want or plan to get into that line of work, and after his marriage he took his wife to Hollywood and tried to re-enter the movie business. His wife grew homesick, and after six months the couple returned to Greensboro, where Johns's father-in-law set him up in the clothing store. In Greensboro the chance for what he had sought as a youth was slight, especially for the son of an immigrant family in the white community. But in the Negro community, Johns could be liked and respected and well known; it is not surprising that he became involved in the problems of the Negro community.

More importantly, Johns is a man of strong emotions, a dramatic, mercurial person who is capable of tears when he is hurt, fierce anger when he sees anyone wronged, and

28

deep friendship and love for those he cares about. When he came to Greensboro and his store started catering to Negroes, he became involved with the people, grew to know them, became friends with many of them. And when he saw the segregation, the injustice, the hatred, he was not a man to let it pass. He wanted to do something. He talked to the students, urged local Negroes to join the NAACP, tried to get someone to test segregation, for Johns himself could do nothing directly. Some feel he acted for the profit motive—it's good business to become involved with your customers—but these people do not know Johns. Those who do know him have never questioned his sincerity, for they feel he has lost too much and has been hurt too often to be acting for profit.

When the four boys left his store that afternoon, Johns had done as much as he could in fighting segregation. It was now up to the students.

As the doors locked at Woolworth's, the boys were still sitting at the lunch counter. Finally, about fifteen minutes after the front doors had been closed, they got up and left by the side entrance. One of them said, "I'll be back tomorrow with A & T College." On the outside they were met by the photographer, and after pictures were taken they returned to the campus.

Mr. Harris called the area superintendent, who happened to be in town that day at another Woolworth's in a suburban shopping center, but the superintendent's only advice was: "Call me tomorrow if anything happens."

2

The First Week

*We haven't refused anybody.
Our girls have been busy and
they couldn't get around to
everybody.*

WHEN WOOLWORTH'S opened for business at 9:30 the
next morning, everything was normal. At 10:00 the students arrived. There were twenty-seven men and four
women, all students at A & T. There had been no mention
yet in any newspaper, but the news had traveled by word
of mouth on the campus. Most of the men were from Scott
dormitory, where the four boys lived. The students, most
of them dressed in coats and ties, had brought their school-
books and they sat down at the counter and started studying. No one from Woolworth's approached them, and no
words passed between students and management. Occasionally a student would ask a waitress, "Miss, may I have
something?" but that was the extent of the confrontation.

In the white community at large, there was little or no
knowledge of the sit-in. In that morning's Greensboro
Daily News no mention of the student action had been
made. The two papers in Greensboro, the *Daily News* and
the *Record*, were owned by the same company, with news
departments in the same buildings on the same floor. But
while the business, circulation, and printing departments
were combined, the news and editorial departments were

31

separate then and competition between the two was strong. The news departments of both papers used the same teletype machines, but that was as close as they came to cooperation. On Monday, Ralph Johns had called Jo Spivey of the *Record*. The *Record* had not told the *News* of the sit-ins.

On Tuesday, however, reporters from both papers, a UPI man (AP was represented by the Greensboro papers), photographers, and television cameramen were present. C. L. Harris stated that no photographs would be allowed —anyone taking them would be trespassing. His announcement did little to deter the news media, and pictures were taken. When asked questions by some newspaperman, Harris would usually say, "No comment."

Several students were interviewed by the press, and one was quoted as saying, "We are prepared to keep on coming for two years if we have to." Another said, "They sell us merchandise from other counters, we say they should serve us at the lunch counter." Ezell Blair Jr. declared that Negro adults "have been complacent and fearful. It is time for someone to wake up and change the situation, and we decided to start here." The press was able to get one statement from Harris: "They can just sit there. It's nothing to me." J. W. Largen, district superintendent of Woolworth's, who was also present that morning, told a reporter, "We haven't refused anybody. Our girls have been busy and they couldn't get around to everybody."

Whites continued to come eat at Woolworth's that day, and although for most of them it was their first knowledge of the sit-ins, no unpleasant incidents were reported. In fact, interchanges between students and customers seemed quite normal—except that Negroes were not served. One student passed the sugar to a white patron who asked for it politely.

A little before noon, Elis F. Corbett, head of the A & T News Information Bureau (he also ran Sports Information and Alumni Relations), came downtown to get some film for the pictures he takes around campus. Corbett is a former newspaperman—he answers the telephone like a movie newspaperman: "Corbett here!"—and is well liked by local newsmen. Corbett went to get his film at the Carolina Camera Center on Sycamore Street, directly behind Woolworth's. Inside, he was joking with the clerks. "Looks like you've got some pictures to take today," one of them said. "Nothing in particular," Corbett commented, and left. He did not know that less than fifty feet away, A & T students were starting what would be termed a revolution.

When Corbett returned to the campus, he found he had missed calls from the wire services, local newspapers, radio stations, and other news sources. In a normal morning, he might receive one call. He returned one of the calls to find out what was up. His first reaction, as he recalls, was shock. Then he reacted like a newspaperman. He picked up his camera and went to Woolworth's.

At A & T, President Warmoth T. Gibbs was in his office when several students came in. Dr. Gibbs is a friendly old gentleman, at the time he was sixty-five, and he liked students to come to his office and talk. These told him that A & T students were staging a sit-down strike at Woolworth's. Dr. Gibbs had heard nothing about it, and his response was, "Is it really so?" And then, "Why?" He says that at the time he could not understand why they had picked Woolworth's—the store did not have a reputation for fine food—but he knew the sit-downs would require

33

Dr. Warmath T. Gibbs, President of A & T at the time of the sit-ins. *Photo: Greensboro Daily News.*

some action by the college and he felt that this was a job for the dean of men. He immediately placed a call to William H. Gamble.

When Dean Gamble heard of the sit-ins, he said, "Let them sit." As long as they were not breaking the law, he saw nothing he could do. Gamble, a light-skinned, youthful Negro, was a quiet-talking person who got along well with the students. He had been dean of men since 1940, and civil rights people regarded him as "straight"—he was for them. He had heard nothing of any sit-in plans, and Dr. Gibbs gave him no specific instructions, other than to express concern that there might be violence. Gamble was left in complete charge throughout the whole period. He wanted it that way: if there was any trouble, he would be blamed and not the president.

The students remained at the Woolworth's counter until 12:30, then left, saying they would return at 2:30. They did not return. Two plainclothes detectives were on duty, but they reported no disturbances. That afternoon, the Greensboro *Record* came out with the first published account of the sit-ins. The lead story on the first page of the second section, the local page, read: "A & T Students Launch 'Sit-Down' Demand for Service at Downtown Lunch Counter." There was a picture of the students at the counter and a one-column story.

That night at the monthly meeting of the NAACP, the local chapter voted to back the students in any way it could, chiefly legally. Earlier in the day, the four boys had been to see Dr. Simkins, who promised them, as he had Ralph Johns, that he would see what he could do personally. Dr. Simkins had just finished reading a pamphlet on the Congress of Racial Equality's work in Baltimore, and he felt it might be able to help. Dr. Simkins, a practical man who seemed little interested in the idealistic aspects of the civil rights question, contacted CORE to see if they would be interested in advising the Greensboro students.

Much emphasis was later put on this move of Dr. Simkins, some writers seeing it as a revolt of the local leadership against the national NAACP, but when Dr. Simkins called in CORE he was making no conscious revolt against the NAACP. He simply believed that the A & T students' protest was too small for the national NAACP, and he was going where he felt he could get the best results. The next week CORE sent a field representative to Greensboro.

That same night some of the students, Dean Gamble, Ezell Blair's father, J. W. Largen of the regional Woolworth's office, C. L. Harris, and others met at A & T to try to solve the problem. Largen wanted Gamble to keep the students on campus, but Gamble said he could not control the private activities of the students. Largen said the decision to integrate would have to be made in Atlanta, the regional office, and he would be glad to have the students go there to discuss the problem. The students said they would be glad to go and asked if Woolworth's would pay their way. Largen said no, and the students replied that they would have to keep demonstrating.

That night the students mailed a letter to the head office of F. W. Woolworth & Co., in New York. The letter was composed by Ralph Johns:

Dear Mr. President:

We the undersigned are students at the Negro college in the city of Greensboro. Time and time again we have gone into Woolworth stores of Greensboro. We have bought thousands of items at hundreds of the counters in your store. Our money

36

being accepted without rancor or discrimination and with politeness toward us. When at a long counter just three feet away our money is not acceptable because of the color of our skins. This letter is not being written with resentment toward your company, but with a hope of understanding. . . .

We are asking that your company take a firm stand to eliminate discrimination. We firmly believe that God will give courage and guidance in the solving of this problem.

> Sincerely yours,
> *Student Executive Committee*
> Ezell Blair Jr.
> David Price
> Joseph McNeil
> David Richmond
> Franklin McCain

David Price was a former employee of Johns and A & T student whom Johns had asked in 1958 to attempt the sit-in. He was no longer in Greensboro at this time but Johns felt his name should be on the letter.

The next morning, Wednesday, February 3, the *Daily News,* somewhat more conservative in its news play than the *Record* and rarely going in for large headlines, finally ran the story of the sit-ins—in the middle of the "local" page. The big stories on the page that day were a traffic jam at the coliseum for a Harlem Globetrotters basketball game, and an influenza epidemic that was sweeping the city. The sit-in story, "Negroes Fail to Obtain Service," read in part: "The dean of men at A & T College is investigating incidents in which Negro students of the college yesterday and Monday occupied seats at a lunch counter of the F. W. Woolworth store here." The story quoted Presi-

37

Sitting in at Woolworth's lunch counter, February, 1960. *Photo:* Greensboro *Daily News.*

dent Warmoth Gibbs as saying, "Another statement will be made once the investigation is sufficiently under way or completed." Dr. George Simkins, who had also been interviewed, had said that although the organization had no previous knowledge of the demonstrations, the local NAACP was 100 percent behind the idea.

Early that morning the four boys went to the Shiloh Baptist Church to use the mimeograph machine. This was the church Blair attended, and he knew that the minister, Reverend Otis Hairston, would let them use the machine to print some instructions for use by the students in the sit-ins. According to Hairston, the boys were very excited but had really no idea what they were doing or how to do it. They had started something with no organization, no planning, and now the whole student body wanted to go to Woolworth's. Hairston advised them to send only enough students to take up the seats at Woolworth's, but he left most of it up to them. He felt, as did many other older Negroes, that this was the students' movement, and he did not want to horn in. But he remembers that whatever they lacked in planning and organization, they made up in momentum. How long this momentum could last, he did not know.

That day students started arriving about 11 A.M. At one time sixty-three of the sixty-six seats were occupied by the students, and more were standing in the aisles to take the place of any who had to leave. The other three seats were taken by idle waitresses, who were having a rather slow morning. Girls from Bennett College were also present, and for the first time Negroes who were not students took part. Around noon several Negroes who worked in the downtown area came in on their lunch hour to help the students. They missed their lunch that day. In the early afternoon three boys from Greensboro College, a white Methodist institution, came in and talked to the Negro students to let them know they were supporting them. The three white students said they believed that white students from other colleges in the area would come and back the Negroes.

Other whites were also present, but they were not there to support the Negro students. Mostly teenage boys or men in their early twenties, these whites stood behind the Negroes. They made comments among themselves, such as "burr-head nigger," not loud but loud enough so that the Negroes could hear. At 1:30 an argument arose between a group of young whites and a Negro; the Negro was quoted as saying, "Come outside and I will take any of you." The police escorted the Negro and the whites from the store. Reverend George Dorsett, Klud of the local Ku Klux Klan, was present.

That afternoon Woolworth's closed the stand-up lunch bar which served Negroes. Harris said that it was not closed and that the waitress was merely relieving a girl at another counter, but another waitress told a reporter that the bar was closed. A Woolworth's representative had arrived from Atlanta, and Harris was keeping in frequent contact with the New York office by telephone.

That day a statement was issued by the North Carolina attorney general, Malcolm Seawell. He said that no North Carolina law prohibited serving members of both races at a lunch counter, but he knew of no law that would force a private business to serve anybody it did not want to. The national headquarters of Woolworth's also issued a statement that it was the company's policy to "abide by local custom." The statement went on to say that if any group succeeded in changing the custom, Woolworth's "will of course go along with that."

In the evening two college officials issued statements.

40

Dr. Harold Hutson, president of Greensboro College, said that the three white students who had supported the Negroes at Woolworth's were acting as individual citizens and were not connected with the college. And Dean Gamble of A & T said that his college had no authority to restrict students' private activities of this kind.

A & T took no official position during the sit-ins, simply stating that it could not restrict students' outside activities. As a state college, A & T was dependent on the North Carolina legislature, and any supporting action on the part of college officials might have cut into the school's appropriations. The college required that the students attend classes (some professors are known not to have kept attendance during the demonstrations), and the school was in close contact with the leaders of the sit-ins, so that it would have knowledge of the students' actions. But this was about the extent of the college's actions except to participate in the different negotiations to try and bring about a settlement.

The school did make one important request: if students were going to participate, no outside organizations should be brought in. A & T wanted the leadership kept among the students, so that they would not become obligated to any organization other than the college—a situation that might have brought the charge that the school was dominated by outside forces.

Thursday morning the *Daily News* carried the sit-ins as its main local story, accompanied by a picture. Out at the A & T campus, there was no other story. As one boy remembered it, "It was like a fever. Everyone wanted to go. We were so happy." A student who went to Woolworth's that day wrote in the school paper about his feelings and experience.

41

After attending a mass meeting in Harrison Auditorium, I was . . . inspired to go down to Woolworth's and just sit, hoping to be served. . . . By luck I was able to get a ride down to the parking lot and there left the car, after which we walked to Woolworth's, read a passage from the Bible, and waited for the doors to open. The doors opened and in we went. I almost ran, because I was determined to get a seat and I was very much interested in being the first to sit down. I sat down and there was a waitress standing directly in front of me, so I asked her if I might have a cup of black coffee and two donuts please. She looked at me and moved to another area of the counter.

The tension was high at Woolworth's as students from A & T, Bennett, and this time Dudley High School, the Negro high school in Greensboro, all sat at the counter. Estimates of the size of the group ran as high as three hundred. But the crowd of white boys—described as "the duck-tailed, leather-jacket group"—was also more numerous. They blocked the aisles and began a counter-sit-in movement by occupying many of the lunch counter stools.

The police report for that morning read: "The tension at that time was already running high. . . . We maneuvered into several potential dangerous situations and broke up the gathers. During the mid-morning, a white boy spilled a glass of coke on the head of a colored student. We are unable to say whether it was accidental or intentionally." Two white youths were escorted out of the store after yelling and swearing. "Nigger" and "burr-head" were favorite epithets. The students ignored the taunts.

At 12:05 a local white man who had been a vocal Nazi sympathizer during World War II and was generally regarded as one of the town nuts came into Woolworth's and started making comments in support of the Negro students to the whites. Police quickly escorted the man out of the store.

With many of the counter seats at Woolworth's occupied by the whites, the Negro students conferred, and at a little after noon, many of them started to march down to S. H. Kress & Co., another variety store on South Elm Street, less than half a block away. They sat down at the basement lunch counter. Some of the white youths followed, and the situation at Kress's became very similar to that at Woolworth's. Police were on duty there also, both plain-clothes and uniformed, and the two detectives present made a report:

> At first the disturbance seemed to be minor. The routine operating procedures of the store and personnel employed seemed to be upset somewhat. However, as the course of the evening wore on, tensions mounted, white students from all the local schools plus outsiders began to agitate these colored people. . . . Again I can say that the situation is highly explosive, agitated by many, many factors, such as radio, T.V., newspapers, and in general, just rowsers. The situation will explode in my opinion if there isn't some decision or clear cut policy made reference handling this situation. . . . The sheer numbers of this crowd should the situation explode is beyond hope of control as to officers.

Back at Woolworth's, things were getting worse. At 1 P.M. three white students from Woman's College, the Greensboro division of the University of North Carolina, came into the store. The three girls, from Florida, Washington, D.C., and London, England, said they "felt it was our

43

moral obligation" to help the Negro students. They began sitting in. The police detective present that day wrote in his report: "It is noted herein that the situation became immediately explosive upon their [the white girls'] joining the colored group and remained that way until the store closed. Their presence among the colored students acted to inflame the feelings of all spectators and also the white students who were there in opposition to the colored demonstration." The police recognized many local troublemakers in the white crowd.

The next morning, Friday, February 5, the Greensboro *Daily News* carried its first editorial on the sit-ins. It was entitled "Leadership at the Five and Ten."

> . . . A time has come for community leadership of both races to assert itself.
>
> . . . . Ultimately, if not solved amicably, this could erupt into something worse, and that will reflect poorly on the community, including Woolworth and the colleges involved.
>
> Much more could be said about the legal, moral and business questions. Legally, Woolworth might eject the sit-downers. . . . But this is a course of action we are sure the management does not want to follow.
>
> Negro patrons occupying seats at the lunch counter have a position which demands consideration. In downtown Greensboro, there are few, if any, restaurants or cafes where they can be served. Resentment against this dearth of facilities is not without justification.
>
> But the way to remedy such a situation is through petition and negotiation, rather than through a sit-down strike. No effort has been made to con-

44

tact Woolworth management about providing such facilities. . . .

There is a proper way to handle such matters, and it ought to be resorted to before something much more serious happens at the five and ten.

On Friday the situation at the variety stores was similar to that of the day before. The detectives on duty arrived about 10 A.M. They reported that "a rough count of fifty white males, mostly the long haired teenaged group, had the majority of stools occupied." Many of the white youths were students from the county high schools, and the Greensboro *Record* in an editorial that day lamented the fact that the county schools that year had not appropriated enough money for a truant officer.

At 10:30 the Negro students started arriving, but they were thwarted in the move to occupy all the seats by the presence of the white youths. The first arrests were reported that day as the police took in one man for assault with a deadly weapon (he was burning a student's coat with a piece of paper), another for drunkenness, and one for disorderly conduct. They were all white. Several whites, both men and women, were escorted from the store for using abusive language. Many things were said to the Negro students, and one observer remembers, "They would take things nobody would take." The newspapers reported that dozens of detectives and uniformed policemen were present.

Other law-enforcement officers were at the stores: constables, elected officials. These men were not connected in any way with the police department, but they could issue warrants for arrest, and some were reputed to have Klan backgrounds. One, Mitch Bell, who escorted several Negroes out of the store, threatening arrest, was seen on occasions conferring with Klan members.

45

The Reverend George Dorsett of the local Klan was again present. He told a reporter he was there "to take care of my men and to keep violence to a minimum." For the most part Dorsett stood in the background and observed, but on this day he was also helping in the counter-sit-in. The usual tactic was to keep the seat until some white person who wanted to eat came in, then relinquish the seat to that person. While Dorsett was sitting, a young white girl came in. Dorsett, in the tradition of the Southern gentleman, politely got up and offered her the seat. She took it, but unfortunately for Dorsett, she was one of the Woman's College girls. She promptly gave it to one of the Negro students.

In the newspaper accounts of that day Dr. Gordon Blackwell, chancellor of Woman's College, made a statement that the role of Woman's College students was "under very careful study and we are extremely concerned about the situation." The head of the North Carolina Association of Quality Restaurants announced that he had advised members to use a trespass complaint if persons refused to leave when asked. A Negro student was quoted as saying, "We don't expect violence, but if it comes we will meet it with passive resistance. This is a Christian movement." And a leader for the group said, "We have some two thousand persons to call on if needed." Along with the white girls from Woman's College, white students from Guilford College, a Quaker school on the outskirts of the city, were also present. A white Bennett student was also in the store.

At about 3 P.M. with approximately 250 to 300 people crowded around the food counter, the situation grew worse. A student photographer from the A & T *Register*, the school paper, came through the crowd with a camera to take some pictures. The white boys started riding him. "Take my pic-

46

ture, nigger." "Let the nigger through, he's a photographer." Someone in the back yelled, "Nigger, I'll give you two peanuts for that camera." He did not sell. The police report for that day noted: "Between 3:00 and 5:00 the tension mounted. There was a great deal of pushing and shoving between the colored and white students as they walked in the aisles." The stores remained open as usual until 9:30 Friday night, but at 5:30 the students left.

At A & T that day the first extra in the history of the A & T *Register* came out, and the front page headlined, "Students Stage Sitdown Demand." A three-quarter-page picture showed students sitting at the Woolworth counter, studying. The paper, usually a biweekly, was printed in Raleigh. But that Tuesday, with a Wednesday deadline for copy, members of the staff had started organizing for a four-page tabloid. When the paper came out on Friday, it was devoted almost entirely to the sit-ins. There was some filler copy on girls' sports and an article entitled "Get to Know the Groundhog," but the staff had managed to cover most developments of the first three days of the sit-ins.

There were interviews with the four boys, first-hand accounts by students who had participated, a wire to the editor from a former student congratulating the students, an editorial cartoon, and a history of protest movements in other cities involving eating facilities. Albert L. Rozier Jr., student editor of the paper and an Army veteran, concluded in his editorial: "The time has indeed come when we must all face up to the facts, and realize that America can not continue its present position of leadership in world affairs with the stigma of race prejudice and discrimination on the one hand, and grin-in-the-face tactics on the other. The season is here now."

That night a meeting, closed to the press, was held at

47

the YWCA: Dr. Blackwell of Woman's College; Dean Gamble of A & T; Dr. Hutson of Greensboro College; Dr. Willa Player, president of Bennett College; F. P. Evans, Woolworth's representative from Atlanta; J. W. Largen, Woolworth's district superintendent, H. E. Hogate, manager of Kress's; Mr. Harris of the local Woolworth's; and two lawyers for Woolworth's. The meeting lasted two hours. Woolworth's again asked college officials to call the sit-ins off, and the officials repeated that they had no control over their students' activities.

Harris recalled later that officials of both white and Negro schools seemed to be behind the sit-ins. The Woolworth's position was, "Why should it be just two stores?" They did not argue the moral rightness of their position, but they felt it was unfair for them as eating establishments to have to integrate while all others in the downtown area remained segregated. Woolworth's was not opposed to integrating if other restaurants and cafes would also integrate. Earlier in the week Woolworth's management had contacted other eating places about the possibility, but the response was negative. The stores felt it was Woolworth's problem exclusively. Blackwell recommended that the lunch counters be closed Saturday to allow things to cool off, but the variety store did not agree. The meeting broke up with nothing accomplished.

That night the students also met to discuss proposals for a truce so that negotiations might go on. They voted not to call a truce for Saturday morning. To those who desired to negotiate, one student replied, "If we negotiate, my grandchildren will still be worrying about that cup of coffee."

Saturday was a warm, sunny day, the type of Saturday in Greensboro that brings people downtown to shop. Many

The sit-in continues at Woolworth's, February, 1960. *Photo: Greensboro News Record.*

people were in downtown Greensboro that Saturday, but most were not there to shop. At 8:30, when Woolworth's opened, Negroes were crowded around the door waiting to come in and take seats. Only a limited number had been sent, enough to get seats, with instructions to call for more if help was needed. Virtually the whole student bodies of A & T and Bennett were willing to come and take part. At Woman's College, Chancellor Blackwell was "strongly urging" his students not to go to Woolworth's, and no white students were seen participating that morning.

By mid-morning walking and standing room was practically nonexistent with people three-deep at the counter and over six hundred crowded into the lunch-counter area. With the largest crowd of the week present, police were calling the situation a powderkeg. Patrolmen and fire inspectors were walking up and down the aisle in front of the counter in an attempt to keep the aisle open. White boys paraded with Confederate flags, some with miniature flags stuck in cigarettes, while Negroes carried miniature American flags. A Negro parading in the aisles with an American flag was jeered by the crowd. A firecracker was thrown, but no one was hurt.

Four whites and three Negroes were arrested. One of the whites arrested was shooting a water pistol; two of the Negroes were drunk, and the other was taken in for fighting. With the crowd of whites growing, the call went to A & T for more students. At about noon, the football team entered. A & T football players have tended to be big (several weighed over 270 pounds and later played professionally), and when they entered wearing their blue letter jackets, it made a visible impression on the crowd. One of the white youths said, "Here comes the wrecking crew!" The tension increased.

50

Others were in the stores that day. One local school-teacher went to see what was going on, but her husband, who was with her, made her leave. He was afraid of what might happen. Dr. Gibbs and Dean Gamble also went to the stores that morning. Gibbs remembers it as the "ugliest situation. . . . The least little thing could have blown up." The two A & T administrators did not remain long. Police Chief Calhoun was also down in the vicinity of the stores that morning, and that was rare for the police chief. Usually he directed all operations from his office, where he could keep in touch with and direct all divisions via his communications system. But this time the chief wanted to see exactly what was going on. He did not like what he saw.

At 1:09 P.M. J. W. Largen took a call at Woolworth's, reportedly from a female, warning him that a bomb had been planted in the basement. Harris climbed up on one of the counters and announced to the crowd that the store was closing, but there was no response. Then two policemen jumped on the counters and shouted that the store had to be evacuated. In a short time, the crowd was out.

There was later considerable doubt in the minds of some people as to whether there actually was a bomb threat. The situation at Woolworth's was such that the slightest incident could have set off a full-scale riot. But Harris did not want to close the store, making it appear that Woolworth's was giving in to a mob. That there was a call and that the caller said there was a bomb is not in doubt, but it was questioned whether the caller was anonymous.

H. W. Kendall, then editor of the *Daily News,* felt that the call perhaps came from some city official who wanted the store closed. He suggested the city manager, General James Townsend (Ret.), or Chief Calhoun. George Roach, mayor of Greensboro at the time, is another who says he has his own ideas about who called in the bomb threat. He never asked who sent it, but later said simply, "I thank God it came." He has also talked about the brilliance of Chief Calhoun in handling the sit-ins. Many others have expressed the same opinions on the bomb scare, but none of these people has any real proof. Harris stoutly denied the call was a fake, and Chief Calhoun said he had no idea who made it. No bomb was found in a search of the store, but it remained closed the rest of the day.

At Kress's that morning, the situation had been the same, but with the closing of Woolworth's, the crowd there rushed to Kress's. The police report reflected the tension:

> Shortly after the noon hour, the tension began to reach the breaking point. The store was overcrowded, especially in the basement section around the lunch counter with both colored and whites. The three ———— brothers, ————, and several other white people were there with the obvious intention of stirring up some type of discord. At approximately 1:30 the crowd kept building, tensions kept mounting, and it was obvious this thing was going out of control. About this time as we understand it Woolworth was closed down by a Bomb Scare, and the entire crowd converged on Kress. Several white people laid down an ultimatum that they were going to close Kress. Gave us a few minutes to negotiate with the manager to see what could be done. Tensions were very high. Silverware such as knives, forks, and spoons was in evidence in possession of both colored and white when the manager announced that the store was closed [in the interest of public safety]. There was evidence of relief on both the colored and the white.

52

Out in the street, the crowd milled around, completely blocking Elm Street to traffic. In front of Woolworth's the Negroes started chanting, "We whipped Woolworth! We whipped Woolworth!" There were some minor disturbances. In about half an hour the Negroes gathered in a group and started to march back to the A & T campus, chanting, "It's all over! It's all over!" The white boys started to follow, but the police blocked off the street and would not let them pass that point. As the group of Negroes passed the King Cotton Hotel, they were pelted with bags of water. Several of the marchers threw stones at the hotel, and a window on the third floor was broken, but the majority continued on.

At about 3:30, H. W. Kendall of the *Daily News* received a call at his home. Kendall, known as "Slim" because of his lanky build, was one of the most respected editors in the state, and had worked as an editorial writer on the *News* for over thirty years. He had gone home early, having written his editorials and arranged the page for Sunday's paper. The caller was Governor Luther H. Hodges: "Slim, I hear you're having a little trouble down there." Kendall agreed. The two talked for a few minutes and then Hodges came to the point. "Some people seem to think I ought to call out the National Guard. Do you think there's any need for troops up there?" Kendall, a slow-talking, introspective man, replied, "Well, Governor, I'm not really on top of the situation like some are. Has the mayor or chief of police asked for troops yet?" Hodges said No. "Well, Governor," Kendall said, "I think that's your answer." Hodges then called the mayor and the city manager, but the response was the same. Troops were not wanted.

53

That night A & T students had a mass meeting. Dean Gamble announced its results: the students agreed to call a two-week recess to give the stores time to set policies regarding food service for Negroes. A truce had been called.

Other statements were made. At Woman's College, Dr. Blackwell said his students had been asked "not to go to the lunch counters," and at Greensboro College Dr. Hutson made a similar statement. In Raleigh Governor Hodges announced, "I have been informed of developments. I have been in touch with local authorities and I am confident they will be able to handle the situation."

Mayor George Roach issued a statement, Greensboro's first official position on the demonstrations. Roach reviewed the facts of the demonstrations and the nationwide publicity surrounding them: "The students have been orderly and courteous and they have received courteous treatment from personnel of the stores, but they have expressed an unswerving determination to achieve their purpose." After reviewing the history of race relations in Greensboro, he made a statement of three points "to explain the official position of the City of Greensboro":

(1) . . . peace and order essential to personal civil rights of any citizen . . . will be preserved throughout the city.

(2) I call upon the leadership of the Negro students and the business concerns involved to place the public interest above personal considerations, even to the extent of forgoing, for a while, individual rights and financial interests, that by doing so a peaceful solution can evolve which will ultimately satisfy these conflicting factors.

(3) I call upon the citizens of Greensboro to support their community leaders . . . seeking a just and honorable resolution of this problem.

That Sunday's Greensboro *Daily News* gave the protests page-one play, headlined "A & T Students Call Two-Week Recess in Protest Here." There was a picture of the crowd outside Woolworth's, and a complete text of the mayor's statement on page one.

Greensboro now had two weeks to find a solution.

3

The Reaction

I'm a Southern girl, but
I'm a thinking girl.

THE A & T STUDENTS were now hopeful that their goal of integrating the lunch counters at the local Greensboro variety stores would be achieved. Nothing more had been expected when Ralph Johns talked with Joe McNeil, nothing more had been hoped for when the four sat down at the Woolworth's counter that Monday. But these freshmen had started something that was not to stop with Woolworth's and Kress's, was not to stop with Greensboro, and the truce that Saturday was to signal the start of the most massive demonstrations in the history of the South, protests that would spread across the nation. The actions of the students in Greensboro had somehow struck a chord that would bring a response from thousands of other college students throughout the country.

It was February, and on the day the sit-ins started, the biggest story on the front page of the Greensboro *Daily News* was the account of an Arab-Israeli border clash. The United States was involved in no military action, and the economy was steady. Elections were coming in the fall, but it was still too early to get excited over Richard Nixon or the multitude of candidates pursuing the Democratic nomination. Racial news had been light; the main news in the Negro press was the election of a new Daddy Grace. When the *New York Times* picked up the Greensboro story on February 3 it was given one paragraph on a back page. The Greensboro sit-ins would not long remain a back-page story.

Nineteen-sixty was a year for the emerging peoples of Africa, a year of independence for the colonial states of the Dark Continent, a year of freedom for 100 million people. Newspapers were filled with stories of the bloodshed in the Congo, but in sixteen other African countries there was little of the tragedy of the Congo, little of the horror. It was also the year of Sharpsville, where blacks, protesting passbook policies of the South African apartheid government, were fired upon by nervous policemen. Seventy-two were slaughtered. Negro students reading about these things were made more aware of them by the presence of African students enrolled in the Negro colleges. At Tuskegee Institute in Alabama, a sociologist discussed the influence of those students on his campus: "The African students talk about the part they are playing in the independence movements of their continent and frequently they reproach American Negro students for not being as aggressive as their counterparts in Africa."

At Negro colleges across the South, a new semester was starting. Fraternity rush was over, exams would not come again until May, and there was time to think about other things. The basketball tournaments for the colored schools were coming up at the end of the month, and the usual enthusiasm was running high. In the first two weeks of February, five North Carolina Negro colleges played the Aggies from A & T College in Greensboro, but these en-

58

counters made other schools aware that something more than basketball was going on at A & T.

The South is almost unique in having colleges for a single race. It is a product, of course, of the society, of segregation, but because of this it is easier for a Negro to get a college education in the South than anywhere else in the nation. Within a ninety-mile radius of Greensboro there are ten Negro colleges, and in the South there are around a hundred. There is a rivalry between these schools, but there is something more: as one student put it, "The kids in the South feel a close kinship to other colleges and small universities, especially the Negro ones, because we feel that their problems are similar."

As the sit-ins continued, other students became aware that the problem A & T was protesting was no different from their own. At Shaw University in Raleigh, North Carolina, one Negro student remembered, "We began to think about it, and the more we thought the more we saw ourselves in relation to it." But they did more than think about it. As Marzette Watts, a student at Alabama State University who was later expelled for taking part in the demonstrations, explained, "When we discovered that the kids in Greensboro had made a move, we felt we were obligated to show our hand. So a few of us got together and decided we would try to organize a little student move-ment." On Monday, February 8, the spread started.

On that day, twenty-six miles away in Winston-Salem, students from Winston-Salem Teachers College, a Negro school, started sit-ins against discrimination in variety stores there. In a manifesto they issued, one of the stated objectives was "to assure the students of A & T and Ben-nett College of Greensboro that they are not alone in their

59

Sitting in at a Winston-Salem lunch counter, February, 1960. *Photo: Greensboro Daily News.*

stand." On Tuesday three hundred seats at lunch counters across the city were closed. Later some of the counters tried to reopen but they closed immediately when Negroes appeared. One drugstore served everybody one day, but the next day it was closed. Woolworth's erected a partition with the sign "Employees and Guests," and the Woolworth's manager was quoted as saying, "It must be an outside element. It irritated our regular customers." One downtown store had twenty-one demonstrators arrested for trespassing.

That same Monday, students from North Carolina College, a Negro college in Durham, also started a sit-in at lunch counters, and these counters were closed. There was a bomb threat, and a brief scuffle took place between the employees of one store and photographers who were attempting to take pictures.

On Tuesday, February 9, the demonstrations started in Charlotte and Fayetteville, North Carolina, where Negro students from Johnson C. Smith College and Fayetteville State Teachers College staged sit-ins. On Wednesday Raleigh was hit as students from the Negro colleges of Shaw University and St. Augustine's College started their protests in the state capital—following a television newsman's announcement that a "careful check" showed Raleigh Negroes would not protest. Over the next few weeks Raleigh had considerable trouble. At one shopping center forty-three students were arrested for trespassing, eggs were thrown, and two white men were sentenced to sixty days on the road for violence in connection with the demonstrations. At the Kress store in Raleigh all the stools were removed, and the segregated sit-down lunch counter was opened as an integrated stand-up counter. There were no objections to Negroes and whites standing up and eating together.

On Thursday, students from Elizabeth City Teachers College in Elizabeth City, North Carolina, and Hampton Institute in Hampton, Virginia, started demonstrating. In Hampton one shop offered to serve Negroes, but on the special menu coffee was $1.00 and hot dogs $1.45. That same Thursday afternoon Negro high school students in High Point, North Carolina, sixteen miles southwest of Greensboro, staged their own sit-ins. High Point had no Negro college, but these younger students, motivated by the same forces that had stirred the college students, followed their example. In High Point, this group was advised by several Negro ministers, but there was less control than in other demonstrations, and there were a number of fights and arrests. On one occasion white and Negro mobs squared off, but serious violence was averted.

In Portsmouth, Virginia, a similar situation developed as high school students began strikes. Here there was little leadership, and the demonstrations became rather aimless. There were a number of fights, and on several occasions near-riots broke out as Negro and white groups confronted each other.

In Chattanooga, Tennessee, high school students started demonstrations on February 14. On February 23, after the students were dismissed, crowds of Negro and white youths gathered; what followed was termed by the Chattanooga *Times* "the most massive racial clash in the history of Chattanooga." The following day thousands gathered in the downtown area, but this time the throngs were effectively dispersed by the police.

These were the exceptions, however, and as the protests spread, the students followed the nonviolent pattern that had been set in Greensboro. The demonstrations continued, spreading to Concord and Salisbury, North Carolina; Richmond, Virginia; and Nashville, Tennessee. But they were not limited to the border states. In Rock Hill and Orangeburg, South Carolina; Atlanta, Georgia; Tallahassee, Florida; and Montgomery, Alabama, students staged protests. In Rock Hill, a new counterprotest technique emerged as the White Citizens Council urged a boycott of any store that did not remain open and segregated. In Montgomery, when students from Alabama State University attempted to obtain service from a lunch counter in the county courthouse, police lined them up and took their photographs. Governor John Patterson demanded their expulsion from school, and the mayor of Montgomery endorsed the governor's stand.

In New York and New Haven, sympathizers picketed the integrated Woolworth's stores, trying to force some national policy change. In Harlem, picketers including actors Ossie Davis and Geraldine Page claimed that 90 percent of the customers were turned away.

As in Greensboro, the spread of the sit-in demonstrations was not limited to Negroes alone. The first Monday of the spread, white students from Wake Forest, a Baptist college in Winston-Salem, participated with the Negro students, and at Durham four divinity students from Duke University were with the North Carolina College students. In the *Daily Tar Heel,* the student newspaper of the University of North Carolina at Chapel Hill, a virtually all-white state university, the editors came out in strong support of the A & T students:

> Currently the students at said school [A & T] are waging a sitdown strike to obtain eating privileges at F. W. Woolworth Store in Greensboro. Their efforts have gained more than a little attention in the state and region. They have even been

63

joined by some white college students from some of the female colleges in the area. They must stick to their guns publicly. Closing the gap between the races will take time, and peaceful perseverance such as the A & T students are showing is just part of the process. We hope they win. We hope they win BIG and we hope they will SOON.

The pattern continued across the South: Negro students protesting, supported by white sympathizers from nearby colleges. And those students who were not in the South and wanted to give encouragement gave support by other means. During these weeks, the A & T *Register* had letters from students all over the country. The president of the National Student Association wrote, "On behalf of the United States Student Association, I would like to take this opportunity to commend you and the students you represent for your courageous actions in connection with the movement that is currently sweeping the South."

In New York City many of the sympathy picketers protesting in front of Woolworth's stores were white. One of the picketers, Mrs. Yolande Betbeze Fox, a former Miss America from Mobile, Alabama, told the press, "I'm a Southern girl, but I'm a thinking girl."

And so, if those who picketed were primarily young and Negro, those who sympathized included a much wider spectrum. Across the nation these young college students, dressed in coats and ties and sitting quietly at variety stores waiting to be served, were awakening fervor for a cause that had perhaps not been seen in the United States since World War II. This one had no advance publicity, no Madison Avenue promotion, no big money behind it, no organization or planning, and yet it was catching the imagination of a nation.

64

Wilma Dykeman and James Stokeley, two Southern writers, were caught up in the spirit of this youthful movement, and they wrote:

> Any American who is weary of what sometimes seems to be an obsessive national preoccupation with inanimate objects—the thrust of a missile, the spread of chromium tail-fins—will find inspiration in discovering throughout the South a people whose obsession has become the spread of democracy, the thrust of an idea.

And even in the cities that were experiencing the sit-ins, editorial support came from many of the local newspapers. The Greensboro *Daily News* wrote that first month:

> It will do no good to assert that local custom, sufficient for fifty years or even twenty-five years ago, must prevail forever. It may not suffice even to fill up the jails.
>
> The idea's moral force—that colored men no longer tolerate being served at nine counters and rejected at the tenth—cannot be denied.

In Winston-Salem after the counters had been closed, the *Journal and Sentinel* spoke out: "It may be wise to keep the lunch counters closed here for the time being. But it is logical to suggest that when they are opened again that they be opened on a desegregated basis." And in Raleigh, the *News and Observer* chided the stores: "You can't have your chocolate cake and eat it too."

And as the sit-ins spread, there was a growing realization that these were more than just a series of isolated racial incidents, that their importance went far beyond obtaining service for Negroes at variety store lunch counters, that they were in fact to be a genuine turning point in the history of race relations in the South. By April *Commonweal* magazine had written, "It seems clear that this 'lunch counter movement' will become a historic milestone in the American Negro's efforts to win the rights of citizenship which are guaranteed him by the Constitution. . . . [It] unquestionably marks a memorable stage in the development of our American culture."

But support for the sit-ins was far from universal, and there were many who opposed the method. The South saw the most opposition, but it was not alone. *The Wall Street Journal* came out against the demonstrations, and the Washington *Star* wrote, "There is both a right and a wrong approach to the problem. And these demonstrations are taking the wrong approach." Many students also opposed the sit-ins and their purpose. In a poll taken at Duke University, about half the undergraduate men favored continuation of segregation policies there, and at Wake Forest, students voted by over a 2 to 1 margin not to integrate. The school paper at Rice Institute in Texas, the *Thresher,* ran an editorial: "As the smoke gradually clears from the blaze of Negro sit-down strikes at lunch counters across the South, one fact stands out more solidly than ever; the Negroes, fighting for rights which they in truth have no claim to, have lost the support among moderates in the South and have done themselves more harm than good."

Many white Southerners still would not believe that the Negro was dissatisfied. When they saw this mass protest spreading across the section, they believed it had to be outside-inspired and planned. Southerners had seen other incidents, such as the Montgomery bus boycott in 1955 and the integration of Little Rock in 1957, that were much more dramatic and had much more publicity, and these had not spread. Many believed the protests to be CORE-inspired, and although, as in Greensboro, the organization usually came in only after the demonstrations had started, its presence led many to condemn the sit-ins. In Congress, Senator Spessard L. Holland of Florida said, "I call attention to the fact that the sit-down raids have been occasioned and fomented by an organization outside the Southland (CORE). . . . [This] could lead to national tragedy."

But for those who continued to believe the sit-ins to be planned and organized by some outside force, the question arose as to why the sit-ins had begun in Greensboro. In Anderson, South Carolina, a Negro newspaper publisher, Davis Lee, had the answer: "The student or youth movement is not a spontaneous rebellion against established customs and practices. It is a well-organized movement. . . . It is apparent that A & T College in Greensboro was selected to kick off the student sit-down movement because three years ago the students there had the courage to boo Governor Luther Hodges when he appeared as a guest speaker."

The incident had happened five years earlier, but it had happened. Students booed Hodges in a 1955 assembly, and it was said that it killed the president, Dr. F. D. Bluford. Dr. Bluford, due to retire that year, lived only a few months after the speech.

Governor Hodges had mispronounced the word "Negro." He had done it three times. The first time there was a rumble in the auditorium, but after the second and third times, the students left no doubt about their feelings as they booed and hissed openly. They did not like hearing Hodges say "nigra." Hodges asked Bluford if he should continue, and Bluford said by all means, but the damage had been done and the governor quickly ran through the rest of the speech.

It was surprising to many outside the college that the students should display their feelings in such a manner to the governor; these particular students had heard and been called much worse. Many white Southerners considered "nigra" a rather liberal term. And these students, usually from the poorer families in the state and thus the first in their families to go to college, should have expected it. They did not, and what they did expect was quite different. During the 1960 sit-ins Albert T. Rozier was to say, "It is too much to expect of any educated man that he accept second-class citizenship in a society such as ours," a sentiment the 1955 A & T students would surely have applauded. These students indeed expected something more now that they had a college education—and here they were, being called by the same old names.

There was another reason why the students felt free to boo, and this had largely to do with the atmosphere at A & T, which had a recent history of similar incidents. Students had booed a trustee—Julian Price, president of Jefferson Standard Life Insurance Company and one of the wealthiest men in Greensboro—when he made a similar slip, and in the late thirties there had been a series of student strikes in protest over administration policies. In 1937 they had boycotted local movie theatres in protest over the deletion from films of certain scenes involving Negroes, stopping only when a theatre brought Fats Waller to Greensboro for a special concert.

These incidents might not have seemed unusual in many undergraduate schools, but this was a Negro college and these schools had not performed the same functions as white schools. One observer of the Negro college has written: "The Negro college student had historically led a relatively sheltered life on the fringes of the white community.

. . . [He] received little encouragement to enter into the affairs of the larger community, and the Negro college became a world unto itself."

A & T was different. Few of the students were sheltered or cut off from the white community. Unlike the sons and daughters of the Negro professional classes who went to schools such as Morehouse and Fisk, these students had to go out in the community and work to keep themselves in college. They would take part-time jobs as porters or bus-boys in downtown stores, or work weekends as yardmen in the white neighborhoods. The very closeness of the school to the downtown area made it unlikely that A & T be a world unto itself.

The policy of the deans, partly out of necessity, was to treat the students like adults, and there was little attempt to control their activities after class. Unlike other Negro schools, no professors lived on campus, and the various school organizations, over eighty by 1960, were almost completely student-controlled. For this reason, some parents did not send their children to A & T, feeling that there was too much freedom for freshmen; they wanted their children to have guidance, knowing the school's large drop-out rate. But for those who stayed an atmosphere developed, an atmosphere that resisted administration interference, an atmosphere in which students could feel free to boo the governor if they disliked what he said, in which four boys could go sit in at Woolworth's without fear of administration reprisals.

It was not that the A & T administration had a liberal or progressive tradition. It was, after all, an agricultural and technical school, and even more importantly, a state school, and there was little inclination on the part of the administration toward liberal thought. There was always

69

the yearly necessity of going to the legislature for funds and appropriations, and any seeming deviation from the accepted white view of the racial issue would not be met warmly by a legislature controlled by rural voters.

It was, in fact, thanks to segregation that A & T was originally founded. In 1889 an Agricultural and Mechanical college for whites (later to become North Carolina State University) had been founded. In order for A & M to receive federal funds under the Morrill Act, it was necessary to have a Negro A & M college receiving equal funds. Thus on March 9, 1891, the General Assembly of North Carolina established the "A. and M. College for the Colored Race." It was provided that the school be located in whatever city or town made a suitable proposition to serve as an inducement to the college, and in 1893, when a group of Greensboro citizens donated fourteen acres of land for a site and eleven thousand dollars to aid in the construction of buildings, the school was established in Greensboro.

In its early years the college was primarily a trade school, and it followed closely the Booker T. Washington ideal of education, turning out worthwhile artisans and workers who would be able to contribute to Southern society. The name was changed, and as A & T it continued to train tailors, shoemakers, mechanics, and other tradesmen along with farmers and technical students.

From 1896 to 1955 the school had but two presidents, Dr. James B. Dudley (1896–1925) and Dr. F. D. Bluford (1925–1955), and these men shaped the school. Both were very conservative (as were practically all Negro college administrators during these years), and Bluford was often described as highly autocratic. He selected his faculty carefully and tolerated little dissent from them. He was accused of firing some for membership in the NAACP, and he supposedly returned about one-half the budget each year to make a good impression on the state legislature.

It is therefore surprising that he gave the students as much freedom as he did. Some have explained it by saying the students would not have tolerated any control, while others say that with students working in the city, there was simply no way to control them. But those who knew Dr. Bluford insisted that he was never antistudent and often used the word "shrewd" in describing him.

But all agreed he would not have tolerated the sit-ins, and in early 1960 many were wondering why his successor and part of the Bluford "team," Dr. Warmoth T. Gibbs, was doing nothing to stop the students.

4

The Response

Realizing the explosive character of the situation and the harm that might be done to the community, I concluded that something should be done.

WHILE THE demonstrations were spreading elsewhere, all activity had stopped in Greensboro, and on Monday, February 8, both newspapers came out with editorials on the situation. The *Daily News* editorial, entitled "Needed: A Just and Honorable Answer," talked about the "Greensboro Spirit":

> Mayor George Roach appealed to the Greensboro Spirit Saturday. . . . The failure of some in the community to sense the deep meaning of this protest delayed action by community mediators almost to the very edge of racial violence. . . . But the substance of his [the mayor's] statement was that Greensboro has the resources to meet this latest impasse, if it uses them properly. We agree. . . .

The *Record* also talked about the mayor's statement, terming it a "masterly appeal for calm and good order." The newspaper implored "the whole community . . . to renew and refurbish the cooperation between the citizens of both races which has done so much to make Greensboro the progressive city that it is in race relations." But many readers questioned whether there was a "Greensboro

Spirit" and whether the city's race relations were progressive enough to solve the problem.

When the results of the 1960 census were released that spring, the *Daily News* headlined them with a page-one streamer: "Population of City Rises to 119,307." This story's play was bigger than that given any of the sit-ins, giving an indication of the city's attitude. The population had grown more than fifty thousand in the decade of the fifties, and the mood of growth with the new wealth it created permeated the city. Greensboro was on the move, and it was proud of the fact and wanted nothing to stop it.

Greensboro, a crossroads fifty miles south of Virginia in the red clay hills of the Piedmont, was created by legislative act in 1807. Located in Guilford County (five miles from the site of the Battle of Guilford Court House, one of the lesser battles of the Revolutionary War), it had been named after the leader of the Colonial forces, General Nathanael Greene. By 1870 its population was only 497, and the town's chief claim to fame was that the carpetbagger Albion Tourgee had lived there during Reconstruction. But Greensboro became a town of the New South, a city of 10,035 by 1900. Its growth was largely attributable to the railroad and that ubiquitous Piedmont Carolina institution, the textile mill. The railroads serving Greensboro became part of J. P. Morgan's Southern Railway System; the textile mills had been started in 1893 by two traveling wholesale grocers, Moses and Ceaser Cone.

The city's biggest growth came during the twenties with a city-limits expansion and a population rise to over fifty thousand. The formation of other mills such as Burlington Mills and Blue Bell, of the Vick Chemical Com-

74

pany, and of insurance companies like Jefferson Standard and Pilot Life, all contributed to its growth.

Greensboro in 1960 was a business city, controlled by businessmen, a city that had five colleges but whose intellectuals had little influence. Business leaders tended to be social leaders, and as in any city of first- and second-generation families, money and place of employment were at least as important as family in gaining social status.

Greensboro had its country clubs and debutante ball (significantly enough, not started until 1951), but it had little of the tradition of the Old South, other than its share of Southern hospitality and graciousness. And, the influx of new people and tremendous growth of the city gave it more of the atmosphere of the North than of a traditional Southern town. This atmosphere in Greensboro was characteristic in much of the state, as has been described by V. O. Key in his *Southern Politics:*

> The prevailing mood in North Carolina is not hard to sense; it is energetic and ambitious. The citizens are determined and confident; they are on the move. The mood is at odds with much of the rest of the South—a tenor and attitude of action that has set the state apart from its neighbors. Many see in North Carolina a closer approximation to national norms, or national expectations of performance than they find elsewhere in the South. In any competition for national judgment they deem the state far more "presentable" than its southern neighbors. It enjoys a reputation for progressive outlook and action in many phases of life. . . .

Of course, Greensboro had many of the Southern attitudes on race, but many in the city prided themselves on their liberal thinking, and the *New York Times* wrote during the sit-ins: "The views of the whites in this traditionally moderate city of 120,000 are mixed and run from what might be called Northern liberal to Southern adamant." Greensboro was one of the three cities in the state which had complied with the Supreme Court's school desegregation decision. Buses, the library, the airport, parks, and the coliseum had all been desegregated by 1960, and Negroes had been on the police force since 1944. The city had been one of the first Southern towns to elect a Negro to the City Council, choosing Dr. William H. Hampton in 1951, and when he died during the second week of February 1960, the local press wrote editorial eulogies, giving him as an example of how race problems should be solved. The *Record* wrote: "We hope his influence and example will be a guiding light for his people."

Racial attitudes similar to those in Greensboro were also widely held through most of the Piedmont and western sections of the state, which helped account for the picture of North Carolina as traditionally moderate. The view was largely a comparative one, for North Carolina, no particular pioneer in racial matters, had gone along with what was necessary and had seen little of the race violence and anti-Negro actions common in other Southern states. The Greensboro *Daily News* mirrored the state's attitude toward the desegregation decision when it wrote: "This state has managed so far in episodes growing out of the Brown decision to keep the courts from breathing down our necks. We have done what we reluctantly deemed necessary, but with full awareness of the need for avoiding court orders and public disorders."

North Carolina did have its Klan, but there was little of the race-baiting and demagoguery found among some of its neighbors and the politics of the state were rather moderate. As V. O. Key wrote, "It has been the vogue to be progressive. Willingness to accept new ideas, sense of community responsibility toward the Negro, feeling of common purpose, and relative prosperity had given North Carolina a more sophisticated politics than exists in most Southern states. The spirit of the state has not tolerated strident demagoguery."

Nonetheless, Greensboro's race relations did have their seamy side. After the *Brown* decision, the school board announced that it would obey the law and follow this ruling. The school superintendent, Ben L. Smith, and the chairman of the school board, D. E. Hudgins, became targets for the letters, phone calls, and general abuse of those who opposed it. When the first Negro entered Greensboro Senior High School in 1957, the only one among almost two thousand whites, she was spat upon and eggs were dropped out of windows on her. As one observer remembers, "She got holy hell." The girl, Josephine Boyd, lasted out the year, but it was six years before another Negro entered the city's white high schools.

The City of Greensboro, which had boasted of its progress in desegregating municipal facilities, had sold the local swimming pool to a private group to avoid desegregating it, and when Negroes tried to play on the municipal golf course at Gillespie Park, the city closed the course and permitted it to turn into a weed patch. Attempts to organize a Negro PTA were discouraged by authorities. At the ball park, Negroes on opposing minor-league teams were fair game for the "good ol' boys" in the third-base bleachers, and the abuse heaped on these players prompted one Greensboro manager to ask if he could present an award to an opposing Negro player at the player's home park for the "almost inhuman treatment" he had received from the fans in Greensboro. It was 1961 before the major-league clubs who had farm teams in the city sent a Negro to the local club.

In 1958 the Guilford County Interracial Commission, in its fiftieth year, was ousted from the Greensboro United Fund after fund leaders decided that some citizens were refusing to contribute because they objected to the group. The annual budget for the United Fund was over $759,000. The Interracial Commission had asked for $250.

The Interracial Commission had been one of Greensboro's early and few attempts to solve its racial problems. In 1957 the commission had attempted to interview businessmen about segregated rest rooms, separate drinking fountains, and employing Negroes in nonmanual labor, but in most cases businessmen would not even see the interracial representatives, much less discuss the problems. There were also some women's discussion groups that considered race problems, but many of the members were afraid to go beyond the discussion stage, and these groups withered. The YWCA was one of the leaders in helping promote communication between the two races, and it was one of the very few places in the city where interracial luncheons and meetings could be held. The Girl Scouts also began a program of discussion of race issues and limited integration in the fifties, but as with all these groups, women were either the only members or the majority.

The Interracial Commission had some male members, but these were usually professors at the local colleges and only occasionally a businessman or professional man of any stature. For this reason, these groups had little effect. The women were usually dismissed as do-gooders. They were told they didn't understand the practical aspects of the race

78

question, and the businessmen, civic leaders, and even the local hate groups largely ignored them.

In the two weeks that followed the declaration of truce between students and stores, Greensboro citizens and others were forming and expressing opinions on the sit-ins. The most common form of expression was a letter to the editor, and at one point the volume of mail became so heavy that the *Daily News* had to write a special editorial on company policy in printing letters and what form they should take. Extra columns of news space were allotted. A large number of letter writers used some biblical reference, either to support or to oppose the students, and many wrote in opposition to the white girls who had participated. One writer suggested the girls "should try to enroll at Davidson, Clemson, or maybe West Point instead of Woman's College." (At Woman's College the parents of a roommate of one of the girls who had taken part in the sit-ins removed their daughter from the school.)

Some writers took fairly courageous stands. Merchant Abe Blumenthal, whose store catered to lower-income whites, asked the readers which they would prefer, "sitting alongside of a well-behaved, nicely mannered, cleanly dressed quiet Negro student or sitting alongside of a filthy dirty, . . . disheveled duck tailed, loud mouthed white rowdy who was served promptly even though his white skin looked as if it hadn't been washed since Christmas." Many of the old-line Southern viewpoints were expressed, including the idea that the Negro was "trying to force himself on the whites. . . . I feel that there are still a great number of Negroes who have pride and are well-bred. They have been

79

taught that they are Negroes and can accept it and adjust themselves to the fact."

There were statements outside the press, also. The Greensboro Council of Church Women voted to back equal race service at lunch counters, while the North Carolina Defenders of States Rights, Inc., issued a statement calling on merchants to preserve segregation. In a speech at Bennett College, Dr. Frederick D. Patterson, former president of Tuskegee Institute and a director of the Phelps-Stokes Fund, answered those people who tried to find subversive meanings in the lunch-counter protest: "The eating in public places by people who are perfect strangers can mean only one thing, and that is that they are both or severally hungry." On February 20, a group of two hundred white teenagers met at Greensboro Senior High School to discuss a youth code. The meeting, arranged by the annually aroused Greensboro parents after the annual arrest of underage teenagers for drunkenness, went beyond the discussion of what time teenagers should go to bed, and these white high school students released a summary statement saying they believed the Negro deserved and should have equal rights.

In other statements, the American Civil Liberties Union criticized the attorney general of North Carolina, Malcolm Seawell, who had suggested that stores had the right to serve whomever they pleased. Seawell, who was running for governor, replied that "it is of the utmost unimportance to me as to what efforts or activities the ACLU may support. If they don't like it, they may lump it." A & T students followed with an open letter to Seawell in which they said that he failed to realize "the vast devastating effect" that arrests of Negroes on trespass charges could have. Seawell replied that "just because they are members of the Negro race they have no rights which are not the rights of other

80

citizens." The *Daily News* then wrote an editorial in which it characterized Seawell as the "attorney general who talks too much."

During the two-week truce and even before, it was apparent that the Greensboro press favored the students' demands editorially, and there was some feeling that this had spread over to the news pages. The relations of Woolworth's, and particularly Harris, with the press during this period were not good, and Harris felt he was "crucified" by the local newspapers. Some believed that his "no comment" attitude and his opposition to the taking of any pictures by photographers made the press more sympathetic toward the students. The local news departments denied this, and there is little indication in the news pages that there was any overt slanting of the news. Generally, the papers were praised for the handling of the sit-ins, and it was felt that objective reporting and the lack of sensationalism by the news staffs helped keep emotions down and permitted an atmosphere in which a solution could be sought. There was no attempt to suppress stories on the protests, although certain requests were made and followed. Harris asked that his store not be referred to as a "five and ten cent store," and Mayor Roach, feeling that his efforts at finding a settlement were being hindered, requested that an enthusiastic *Daily News* reporter be asked not to follow him everywhere he went.

Since the 1954 *Brown* decision, the general editorial policy of the *Daily News* had been to favor keeping the peace and following the law. The editorial departments of the *News* and the *Record* were separate in 1960, and there was no company editorial policy. But the two papers generally followed the same pattern, although the morning paper was usually considered the more progressive and influential.

There was a strong sense of community responsibility on the *News,* and this feeling and the desire to keep the peace guided the paper. Almost from the beginning the editorial pages of both papers supported the students, although not without some reservations. The *Daily News* recognized the position of the Negroes in its first editorial but questioned their tactics. The *Record* in its initial editorial on February 4 seemed almost completely opposed to the sit-in tactic:

> [The sit-ins] served the cause of race relations badly. . . . It was an attempt to force an issue by public demonstration. Furthermore, it is the sort of incident that an overt act may turn into something more serious. Undoubtedly the students' "Sit-down" will be cited by some persons as evidence that the Negroes are pushing for social privileges as well as legal rights. There have been other indications of that purpose.
>
> The white leadership of the community can ill afford to be passive and indifferent under the circumstances. There is a dangerous vacuum in the relations between the races, we fear.

Albert Rozier in the A & T *Register* took the *Record* to task for the editorial:

> We agree with the local daily's stand that a dangerous vacuum DOES exist here in so far as race relations are concerned, but why have they, as guardians of the most important medium of expression and perpetuation sat so idly by and permitted the creation and continuation of this acknowledged empty space.

But after the first week, there seemed rarely a time when the two papers were not solidly on the side of the students.

82

A national magazine writer during the crisis termed the papers "influential and moderate."

During the two-week truce, both variety stores had signs on the counters saying "Closed in the Interest of Public Safety," and at Woolworth's the seats were removed and the counters used to display rugs. Both Negroes and whites sent scouts to check the two stores, and three Negroes came in and had their photographs taken in front of the Woolworth's counter. Police reported that a white male entered Woolworth's wearing a long, heavy black coat and sun glasses on a particularly warm day, and one of the Woman's College girls who had participated in the sit-in also entered wearing a disguise. Newspaper stories said Woolworth's officials in New York were contemplating a proposal for total integration of lunch counters in North Carolina only, but apparently this was just a rumor, for a confidential report had Harris traveling to Atlanta on February 19, returning the next day saying the regional office had told him it would not integrate any lunch facilities in the region. The general company feeling was that the movement would lose momentum—all the stores had to do was wait it out and reopen when Negroes tired of demonstrating. The New York office told Atlanta that it would not interfere with regional segregation policies even though the New York store managers, hit by pickets and boycotts, were urging the company to force integration.

Also during these weeks different claims were being made as to who had first had the idea for the sit-ins. NAACP sources said that Negroes in several parts of the state had been discussing sit-ins for some time, and at North Carolina College in Durham, A & T's chief athletic rival, Reverend Douglas Moore said Durham was to have been the first city hit by the sit-ins: "It was felt that it would be easier to integrate stores in Durham because the merchants would not want the publicity attendant to a long boycott. They are seeking trade and the city is seeking more companies for the research triangle and some thought they might be pushovers." He went on to say that students had been mapping plans in December and that it was common knowledge on Negro campuses. It was, however, not common knowledge on the A & T campus.

On February 21, the truce was up. That Sunday's *Daily News* headlined, "A & T Students Drop Sitdown Protests; Plan Negotiations." The story reported that the Student Executive Committee for Justice would pin their hopes on the use of "peaceful channels of negotiations." Mayor Roach announced that the student statement "creates the proper atmosphere under which . . . a solution may be found." The *Daily News* commented editorially on this "act of maturity."

> Whatever "spirit of ultimatum" had been created by the protest . . . has been removed.
> But ultimate responsibility lies with the community. Greensboro has a deep reservoir of faith, understanding, and good will. It has risen to the occasion many times in the past; it can rise again.

But if Greensboro did have a "deep reservoir of faith, understanding, and good will," and if it had "risen to the occasion many times in the past," there were serious doubts that it could rise again—considering the lack of anything constructively accomplished during the two-week truce.

The main problem was leadership. The mayor in his February 7 statement had said that Greensboro was "singularly blessed with good municipal leadership," and the

84

Daily News had editorialized during the two weeks that "The next weeks must not be idled away. . . . Let Greensboro's leadership demonstrate its competency to find a solution which will combine the fairness of moral justice with the salutary qualities of good business and practicality. It can be done!" But the question arose whether Greensboro's leadership was capable of doing anything. The director of information of the Southern Regional Council, who was traveling through North Carolina cities during this period, wrote, "One of the lasting impressions gained is the inability of the white leadership to understand and effectively solve the problems arising from the Negro's desire for status as a first-class citizen." The leadership that the mayor and press were talking about was Greensboro's past leadership, but Greensboro's pattern of leadership in 1960 had changed, and it was not that of earlier years.

Since 1921 Greensboro had been governed by the city council–city manager form of municipal government. The day-to-day decisions were made by an appointed city manager with the elected seven-man council determining policy and advising the manager. The mayor was usually the City Council member with the highest number of votes. In the early years of the council, many of Greensboro's leading citizens had been elected to it—two Cones of Cone Mills, the president of Jefferson Standard Life Insurance Company, the owner of the newspaper and many other prominent men—but by the 1950's fewer of these men were taking part in city government. Lawyers with unpromising practices, insurance salesmen, real-estate men, bondsmen, lesser corporation officials, and others were becoming more and more common on the City Council, with a proportionate lessening of business leaders and the economic elite.

The city, run by a very effective city manager, operated smoothly and efficiently, but it did not have the prestige of earlier years. More importantly, it did not have the influence or power to make people act.

In the weeks following the truce, the newspapers reported rumors of various meetings being held throughout the city, but when Mayor Roach was questioned, he said he had no plans to bring the subject before the weekly City Council meeting. He also said he had not been involved in any efforts toward reaching a settlement of the issue. Others who might have been able to influence the situation seemed to be doing nothing. The Chamber of Commerce had discussed the problem but they questioned whether the sit-ins were really their concern. Executives of many large companies in Greensboro felt it was not a community matter, and leading merchants still expressed the belief that the problem was the variety stores' exclusively. In the A & T *Register* of February 26, Albert L. Rozier wrote, "Students here hope only that they have not overestimated the good will and understanding of the thinking people of Greensboro," but there was every indication that they had.

At Woolworth's and Kress's, the counters reopened on February 23, and although many white and colored observers were present, no trouble was reported. On the twenty-fourth, there was another bomb threat, this time from a Negro, but no one in the store other than Harris knew of it. The basement was cleared for a short time, but no bomb was found, and business resumed as normal. In the kitchen, the situation was tense as the Negro help slowed down their work to almost half pace and would not speak to anyone unless directly asked a question.

Finally on February 27, almost a month after the start

86

of the sit-ins, the first apparent concrete action was taken as the mayor announced the forming of the Mayor's Committee on Community Relations. City Councilman E. R. Zane was appointed chairman. Of the eight other members, two were from the City Council: David Schenck and Waldo Falkener; three from the Chamber of Commerce: Bland Worley, Howard Holderness, and W. M. York; and three from the Merchants Association: O. L. Fryman, Arnold Schiffman, and James A. Doggett. Falkener was the only Negro.

At the meeting in which the mayor announced the forming of the committee, Zane asked the citizens of Greensboro to send the committee their opinions on the students' demands so that some general community consensus could be established. He also made a formal statement:

> I am confident that those of us who have lived steeped in the customs and traditions of our beloved South fully understand and appreciate the many delicate and provocative questions which will arise in undertaking a solution of this problem. Nevertheless, I am convinced that the people of Greensboro, both white and Negro, with the exercise of patience, tolerance, and understanding of the difficulties involved, will, under conscientious and dedicated leadership, produce a reasonable solution acceptable to the majority of our people and establishments involved.

As the meeting closed, Mayor Roach turned to Zane and said, "God be with you."

During the first week in February many people went to the variety stores. There were, of course, the Negroes, the white toughs, and the curiosity seekers. Ed Zane went

87

to Woolworth's the first week, deeply concerned, and when he saw the seriousness of the situation he knew something had to be done. More important, he saw that nobody was doing anything. He wrote to the president of his company, Burlington Mills, the following memorandum:

> Last week, after thorough investigation I ascertained that none of the agencies wrestling with the "lunch counter problem" had reached any conclusion or had any prospects for a solution. Realizing the explosive character of the situation, and harm that might be done to the community, I concluded that something should be done. . . .

Ed Zane did something, and Greensboro's response can be in large measure credited to him.

Ed Zane was born in 1899 in the little town of Arlington, Tennessee. He was the son of a cattle buyer, and there was little extra money in the household. In 1917, ten days after the United States officially entered World War I, Zane enlisted in the Army. Discharged in November 1919 in Washington, D.C., Zane did not return to Tennessee. Instead he worked around Washington until he had enough money saved to enter Georgetown University. He eventually received his LL.B. degree there, and then went to Pace Institute in Philadelphia, where he received his master's in accounting. He returned to Tennessee and set up his own accounting firm, and in 1929, when the city of Greensboro advertised for an out-of-state accountant to audit its books, Zane came to the city to do the job. He eventually settled in Greensboro, and by 1946 employed over forty persons in his own firm. In that year, however, he sold it and went to work for Burlington Mills as a financial consultant and special tax counsel. He had started advising

Burlington and its president, J. Spencer Love, in 1929, when the textile firm was very small. Zane advised the company on all its acquisitions and mergers, and by 1960, its name changed to Burlington Industries, Burlington was the largest textile concern in the country.

It would be very difficult to imagine two more dissimilar men than Ed Zane and Ralph Johns, the two white men who played the most important roles in the Greensboro affair. They know each other only slightly, and their estimation of each other is not high; yet one is struck by something very similar in these two. Zane, the short, balding accountant, is a quiet but effective talker, and he has little of the dramatic flamboyance of Johns. It would be hard to see him as the "world's greatest gate crasher," or a movie actor, or putting signs in front of the Burlington Industries building saying, "Love thy neighbor," or "Segregation is evil," or "Special for today: Faith, Hope, and Charity." But there is a similarity, and in talking to the two men, it comes out, overshadowing all their differences. Ralph Johns and Ed Zane both have strong convictions, along with the rare quality of standing up for what they believe.

Like Johns, Zane is a religious man, and although he expresses his religious feelings quite differently, they are strong ones. Zane will say quietly that if one-third of the people who professed to be Christians practiced Christianity, the world would be a different place. In 1961, when a group of Negroes tried unsuccessfully to gain admittance to one of the services of the Methodist church Zane attended, Zane resigned from that church.

Of the 1960 sit-ins, Zane has said, "My feeling in the whole situation was motivated by a strong sense of injustice." His concern did not arise from any specific feeling

89

Ed Zane, City Councilman at the time of the sit-ins. *Photo:
Greensboro Daily News.*

about Negro rights; it was the concern he would exhibit
for any victim of injustice. This particular kind of injustice,
of course, was built into the whole Southern system, and
Zane recognized the hypocrisy of the separate-but-equal
doctrine. "You've got to look at the nation, the Declaration of Independence, the Constitution. Discrimination just
won't go." He also has said that if segregation were written
into the Constitution, he would have to accept it. But it
wasn't, and he says, "As a citizen, I felt the Southern system
was incompatible with the national system of government.

90

I didn't propose to stand by. Every citizen has an obligation."

On Saturday, February 6, the week the sit-ins started, Zane went to see Mayor Roach. With him he had his resignation from the City Council and a statement. He had been to the Woolworth's store and knew something had to be done. He was going to try to form a committee of leading citizens in Greensboro to meet with the students and store owners and work toward a solution. During the week neither the mayor nor the City Council had issued any statements on the situation. The city had taken no official position and Zane did not see how he could take unilateral action and at the same time remain on the City Council. His only choice, as he saw it, was to resign so he could be free to form some sort of effective committee. This was no grandstand play to try to force the mayor to action, but the only way Zane could see that might bring results.

Zane understood some of the difficulties Mayor Roach was experiencing. Community sentiment had not developed to the point that the mayor could take a clear-cut stand, and he was under tremendous pressure to do nothing. Many townspeople thought the thing would simply pass over, and they did not want the city to become involved. With Greensboro's city-manager form of government, the job of mayor was neither a full-time nor a well-paying position; and Roach, who had his own local realty company, could be seriously hurt financially if he took a position that would bring a violent reaction in the community.

Zane knew this, and he also knew his own position as an officer in Burlington Industries was safe. As a consultant he was not a regular salaried employee, and he could act with a good deal of independence. More impor-

91

tant, Burlington had always backed him in community affairs. He was a close associate of the president, J. Spencer Love, who supported Zane throughout the whole affair. Early on, Zane received a memorandum from Love: "Congratulations and thanks on continuing to take the leadership in the lunch counter situation problem. Please consider me in reserve, and if there is any way you know of that I can be helpful, let me know." Thus, when Zane went to see Mayor Roach, he was not only willing but quite able to take action.

George Roach is a large, friendly man with a folksy manner and an easily identifiable North Carolina accent. At the time of the sit-ins he had been on the City Council since 1955. In 1957 he received the most votes and was chosen mayor. A popular mayor, he worked closely with the city manager, General James Townsend. His official duties, other than presiding at council meetings, were to represent the city in such things as ribbon-cuttings, the giving out of keys to the city, and the proclaiming of special days. He enjoyed this type of duty. The sit-ins were something new.

When Ed Zane presented his resignation, Mayor Roach did not accept it. If he had been reluctant to take action before, he no longer hesitated. He was not going to let all leadership slip from the hands of the City Council, and he was not going to let Zane, one of the ablest councilmen, resign. He agreed to let Zane form his committee, but it was to be the Mayor's Committee, giving official city approval to efforts at settlement. The statement that Zane had been prepared to release to the press announcing his unilateral attempt to find a solution was slightly altered, and the mayor released it as his own statement. The City of Greensboro had taken a stand.

George Roach. Mayor of Greensboro at the time of the sit-ins.
Photo: Greensboro Daily News.

In the three weeks between the mayor's statement and
the announcement of the forming of a committee, Ed Zane
had been hard at work attempting to bring about a settlement. He met with Dean Gamble, interested members of
the A & T faculty, business leaders in the colored community, and members of the A & T student body. He
talked with the Negro students at a meeting held at the
Hayes-Taylor YMCA, the local Negro Y.

93

My approach with the student body representatives was concentrated towards directing their attention to the fact that the method they had initiated for the attainment of their objective was wrong and in direct violation of the owner's legal rights; driving home the principle that moral privileges cannot be obtained by force or intimidation, but must be secured through the medium of orderly negotiations, reason, and mutual respect.

The student body representatives agreed with my reasoning but would not make a decision until the matter was referred to and approved by the student body.

The student body agreed to discontinue the sit-down method and wait and see how the white community acted. This is what Zane had wanted, for it gave his committee time to work out a solution. Five days later came the meeting that announced the forming of the Mayor's Committee, and the press applauded the action. Greensboro was apparently ready to solve its problems.

5

The Four

It was a wonderful year.

FOR FOUR freshmen at the North Carolina Agricultural and Technical College, the spring of 1960 was a unique experience. It was everyone on campus speaking to them, people in lunch lines giving up their places to them. It was every fraternity on campus issuing bids, and newspapermen asking for stories and interviews.

In the fall they had been ordinary freshmen, somewhat lost among the three thousand other students. There was nothing to distinguish them. None of the four played any organized sports or belonged to a fraternity, but the four did form a very close friendship. Joseph McNeil of Wilmington, North Carolina, had not known the others when he came to A & T. His roommate was Ezell Blair, Jr., and Blair had gone to Dudley High School in Greensboro with David Richmond and Franklin McCain, who roomed together one floor up in Scott Hall. The four began to do everything together. At night they would sneak beer into the dorm and sit around and talk. The discussions usually took place in the room of McNeil and Blair, and the other two would come down to talk. They talked about many things, but they were Negroes and they discussed most often subjects like the rights of man and what it meant to be black. The discussions often went late into the night, and the two from the floor above sometimes fell asleep in their friends' room. Like other freshmen before them, they talked about changing the world. They thought they could.

Their talking went further than this, and they began wondering if they were not just like so many other people who as McCain recalled, "talked a lot about problems, made a lot of noise but never did anything. So we wondered about this thing. Who's worse off—the people who aren't aware enough to do anything about problems, or people who are aware enough but never take any action. We really didn't want to put ourselves in the same category as those who talk but never act, so we said, let's *do* something."

But there was nothing, even later, that anyone could recall which seemed to set them apart, to indicate that these four would start anything that would have such a profound effect. Only Joseph McNeil had been involved in any similar situation before. In his home town of Wilmington, local Negroes had boycotted a soft drink firm when he was in high school, but this experience had given him only an idea of what could be accomplished. McNeil was the smartest of the four; he was a physics major, and the other three, not unintelligent themselves, talked about how smart McNeil was. David Richmond could never remember McNeil's being stumped by a teacher's question in class, and of the four his grades were least affected by the time spent with the sit-ins that spring.

Even Ralph Johns, who had asked McNeil to test Woolworth's did not think he would act. On the day in December when McNeil left Johns's store after promising Johns he would test Woolworth's, Johns said as much to

David Richmond. *Photo: Greensboro Daily News.*

Dorothy Graves, the Negro woman who had worked in his store since the early fifties. "Just like the rest," he said. Dorothy agreed. "Yeah, he ain't comin' back."

David Richmond probably would have seemed to be the least likely to start the sit-ins. Richmond, a quiet, guarded talker of slight build, frankly admitted he didn't like crowds and that he didn't like to get up in front of people and talk. In the eighth grade, he had run out of an assembly. Standing in front to address the student body, he could not give the speech and had run off in tears. But he did not run when the crowd spouted taunts at his back as he sat at the Woolworth counter.

Franklin McCain weighed over 200 pounds, and at 6'2" he towered over the other three. But McCain was also quiet, and played on none of the athletic teams, preferring the companionship of his friends. Yet it was McCain who provided the final impetus to go to Woolworth's, for when he asked the others, "Are you chicken?" they could not answer negatively.

Ezell Blair, Jr., also seemed an unlikely candidate to start massive social change. The smallest of the four, he was described by those connected with the sit-ins as the "little brother" type. His main characteristic seemed to be that he talked a good deal, and in fact, many people felt the little freshman was only a chatterbox, and dismissed him as immature. As a boy, Blair had delivered newspapers, and on one occasion a group of white boys took them away from him. When he went to the mother of one and asked her to get the papers back, she began cursing him and threatening to have him sent to jail. But an incident such as this could not have been unusual for a southern Negro boy at the time, and Blair's involvement can probably best be explained through his family.

98

The night of January 31 the four boys had gone out to Blair's home. Ezell's father, a strong-willed, authoritative man, taught industrial arts at Dudley High School. He made an impression much different from that of his son, and it seemed natural that if the boys were seeking the advice of an adult they should turn to this man. Ezell Blair, Sr., was a realist—he had lived too long in the South to be anything else—and he quite frankly doubted that the boys could accomplish anything by trying to get service at Woolworth's. He made no attempt to dissuade the boys, but simply said, "If that's the way you feel, go ahead."

He too had been in Woolworth's and was well aware of their policy, but he had once actually gotten service at the lunch counter. The day after Thanksgiving, 1959, following Greensboro's annual Christmas parade, Blair and his youngest daughter entered Woolworth's and took a seat at the counter. His daughter, unaware of the local customs, had said she was hungry, and Blair, Sr., was tired from standing up for the parade. The two of them sat down. One of his students was behind the counter that morning and when Blair asked for a sandwich she got it for him. She was perfectly aware of the store's policy, but Mr. Blair was "the type of teacher that when he asked you to do something you did it." Soon one of the assistant managers came rushing over to tell Blair that he would have to go to the stand-up counter. Blair's reply was, "I'm doing just fine," and the two continued eating. After finishing the sandwiches, they left.

As the sit-ins grew and his son's name received more publicity, Blair's wife worried about job reprisals—she, also, taught in the local schools. Blair told his wife that if that was all fifteen years of working in the school system meant, he would be glad to get out.

99

Franklin McCain. *Photo: Greensboro Daily News.*

By the end of the day on February first it was really all over for McNeil, Richmond, McCain, and Blair. They took part in everything, were active participants in all discussions and negotiations, but it no longer mattered who had started it or what their reasons were. The four had begun something that would go past any individual leaders, and they knew it. Joe McNeil said, "The movement picked up such strength that personalities were overlooked—that was a good thing, that the meaning of the movement was more important than personalities." It was just that, a movement, and by the third day there were problems of limiting the sit-ins to just the number of demonstrators needed to fill the stools.

When the four sat down, they did so at a time and in a climate that were near perfect. The Negro himself was mentally set to do something about segregation, and such incidents as Montgomery and Little Rock had helped pave the way. As one student remembered, "We had been ready to do something like this for a long time." Another recalled, "I had expected a movement, perhaps not in this form, but with the same sort of 'something's gotta give' that burns in the hearts of most southern Negroes." If the Greensboro sit-ins had not taken place, undoubtedly some other racial incident would have come along to trigger mass protests. It might have been a year or only a week. But Greensboro happened, and it proved the catalyst.

The four boys also sat down at the Woolworth counter at a time when the world situation was relatively stable, when there was little news to distract readers from the sit-ins. They sat down in a moderate Southern city, conscious of its image and unwilling to have the students arrested or inflict violence on them. If for some reason the students had not been allowed to keep sitting in those first

101

few days, there is a good possibility that nothing more would have happened. But they were able to keep sitting long enough to make others aware of what was happening —and even then it almost was not long enough. As one student in Raleigh recalled, "February 1 . . . had been passed by a week or more before most of us realized that the persistence of the Greensboro students was sparking the nucleus of a gigantic movement with mass appeal."

More important than the time and the place of the Greensboro incident, however, was the form it took. Here was a protest against one of the most obvious forms of discrimination, in stores that invited Negroes to shop. And it was a protest that enabled Negroes to express discontent in the non-violent pattern set by Martin Luther King, Jr. in Montgomery in 1955. The inconspicuousness that nearly caused the sit-ins to be overlooked was also part of its appeal: this movement had no charismatic leader and needed none; sitting in was something almost any group of Negroes could do with little planning. It was a movement primarily of the young, a group that had the time and the desire to protest. And it was evident that these protests were definitely going to accomplish something. As the Southern Regional Council reported that first month, "The sit-in demonstrations . . . have spread with such contagion as to make brightly clear that the South is in a time of change the terms of which cannot be dictated by white Southerners."

The four originators were not forgotten, far from it. By the end of the first week they were celebrities on campus. Across the nation they became known as the Four Freshmen, and the honors began to come in. For them that spring was a time for classes to be forgotten, ROTC drills missed; a time to bask in the glory of something they still

Weren't sure of. In the campus newspaper, an English professor, Dr. William H. Robinson, wrote a poem for the demonstrators:

"To the Black Lady Lovers of the Sit-in Demonstrations" (For my students who've asked "What were those knights of old really like?")

Now you know, weary of King Arthur
Headless men and knights of green
How it is:—
How a thick-lipped farm boy mounts a charger
Of neighborhood marked down shoes,
Dons armor of denim shirt and khaki pants,
Spears heaven with a placard sword,
And—wearing day-after-tomorrow in his heart—
Gallops up and down the public length
Of venerated lunch counters—
Look at this black prince of a man!
Oh, enviable ladies, chant a new war song
That drowns out, "Negro, go home."
Sing "Vinpity-bop skiebam-bam!!"
That's cool enough; now once again—
And kiss the dragon's spittle from their backs,
These brand new knights with derivative names:
Sir Booker T. Smith, Knight George Washington
    Jones;
Hold them, ladies, in the jail of your trust
That will rust away the ironmost of bars;
These things will warm the bone-cold winter
Coming raging from the dragon's mouth.
Black ladies, Dame Susie Mae, Queen Willie Jo,
On your summer knees in the Jersey or the Bronx,
Or whatever kitchen ladies must apprentice in,
Understand that unaccustomed, harsh blue-eyed
    look:

Joseph McNeil, left, with others at the Woolworth's lunch counter sit-in.
Photo: Greensboro News Record.

It's hard to know King Arthur's dead;
Harder to know who's employing whom and for
    what??

The four had become symbols for the sit-ins, but even
for symbols there are pressures, and some were beginning
to be felt. The newsmen and awards were problems, and
of the four, only Blair, Jr. really liked to stand in front of
audiences and accept awards and make speeches. His
father worried that his grades would fall, and they did, but
he managed to keep up well enough. David Richmond
became so wound up in the civil rights movement that
spring that his schoolwork seemed to receive little attention. One of his professors asked him what he was doing
in college. He also told Richmond that the problem of discrimination and injustice had been with the Negro for
hundreds of years and would continue to be a problem long
after the one year Richmond would be at A & T if he
didn't shape up. Franklin McCain also had his problem
with the pressures, and his work, too, fell off. Of the four,
only Joe McNeil seemed able to keep up and still remain
involved.

And if their time in March had been spent primarily in
negotiations and discussions, the demands on their time and
involvement increased when it was announced on March 31
that negotiations had failed.

6

The Failure

After two hours and fifteen minutes of discussion, I was unable to break down their adamant stand against any form of change in present policy.

ON FRIDAY, April 1, at 1 P.M., James L. Stover, an A & T senior, took a seat at the lunch counter at Woolworth's. C. L. Harris came up to Stover and spoke to him. "I'm not going to serve you. You can sit there till doomsday. I wish you would leave. You're jeopardizing ever having Negroes sit there and get served." Other Negroes took seats, and as each did, a waitress came up and told them, "We don't want to serve you. Will you leave?" They did not leave. The seven-week truce was over.

That same afternoon, the committee had reported back to the mayor. Their efforts at settlement had failed. They had advised integrated seating with a small section for whites only, but this had met "a stone wall of opposition from store managers."

In the morning A & T and Bennett students had held a meeting attended by twelve hundred in which they voted to resume their sit-ins and to place pickets outside the variety stores. Pickets were limited to five at each store. In the afternoon, neither students at the lunch counter nor those on the outside picketing would talk to reporters except to say that they were returning to keep the situation before the public eye.

Pickets at the S. H. Kress store, April, 1960. *Photo: Greensboro News Record.*

Ezell Blair Jr., in an earlier newspaper interview, had said: "Some Negroes say we're moving, but not fast enough. I say if it takes two or maybe three months to gain equal service with the white people in a chain store that has a hundred years of history behind it, we've done something big." But after seven weeks it seemed that Blair's "two or three months" would accomplish little. The students were impatient for results. At A & T, Albert L. Rozier Jr. wrote in the *Register* of April 1, "It can never be said of the A & T students that they did not allow ample time for a solution favorable to these students."

During the four weeks after appointment, Zane and his committee had not been idle. They had held countless meetings with students and the management of both the variety stores and other eating establishments. They met with business leaders to apprise them of the situation, and held other informal meetings. The committee was vigorously supported by the newspapers, and its request for letters to determine community sentiment was well publicized. The papers had run several articles and editorials on the need to determine the sentiment, and the *Record* had editorialized, "Speak now or forever hold your peace."

Many groups were speaking out. The Greensboro Ministers Fellowship on March 2 had stated, "We consider it a matter of conscience that we invite the citizens to embrace a pattern of inter-group relations with that level of moral maturity which would call for equal treatment of all customers." The Greensboro Methodist Fellowship also came out in support of the students: "We would not be offended in the least should they be served at lunch counters. In fact, our Christian sensitivity would be offended if they were not served." And a small group of whites, many of them members of the old Interracial Commission, went to A & T to reassure the students that some whites were supporting them.

And yet it seemed as though most of Greensboro really didn't care. Harry Golden wrote in early March: "The reaction of the white people has been significant. Most of them do not seem to care what is going on at the dime stores." Greensboro was no different. The city seemed more interested in the fact that sixteen inches of snow was on the ground, the most in twenty years, and that the Ringling Brothers circus was coming and was to be televised nationally from Greensboro. The city's new ice-hockey team was averaging almost 3,000 a game in attendance.

The request for letters by the committee had resulted in 2,063 communications. Many were pleased with that large response, and some out-of-state newspapers commented favorably. But Ed Zane confided in a private letter, "I am terribly disappointed with the public response, both white and Negro." Of the replies 1,501, or 72.8 percent, favored equality of service on some basis, while 562, or 27.2 percent, were opposed to any change in the stores' policy. Of the 562 opposing replies, 200 were mimeographed postcards that were received by the committee on the same day. Zane wrote privately, "I cannot help but agree with the operators that so meager a response does not establish a definite community desire to change existing customs. . . . I have not given up, but I am afraid public complacency, as usual, will defeat the efforts of the committee to resolve this problem in a peaceful manner."

One of the problems the committee faced was itself, for its members were not in complete agreement as to purposes or goals. There had been some difficulty at first in getting members for the group, and feelings on the race issue were divergent. One member recalls that there was no strong feeling that the two stores should integrate, and at least one member was somewhat opposed. Ed Zane said quite frankly that the committee as a whole would have failed, that when the chips were down the majority just didn't want to integrate, and it seemed to be the feeling among some that the Negroes were "going too far." Committee members such as Bland Worley saw the situation chiefly as a community matter and felt the two variety stores should not be singled out. He wrote a letter to Zane on this point:

> The news item in Monday night's *Record* indicated that our committee was interested in finding out the opinion of the citizens of Greensboro regarding the integration of services at Kress and Woolworth.
>
> I would suggest very strongly that we discontinue any reference to the two stores, as the problem is not limited to them. I personally feel that we render a great disservice when the press indicates our committee is considering the situation that exists at these two stores only. I am also afraid that we have little chance of getting the cooperation of these two merchants in any solution that may be reached, unless this can be made a community matter rather than a matter of these two particular stores.

Worley was correct when he saw the problem as a community one, but many of the other eating establishments did not, and the committee found it difficult even to get representatives of these places to attend meetings.

Any differences the committee might have had were overshadowed by Ed Zane, who, as chairman, dominated the group. What Zane thought was generally taken as the Committee's thoughts. He agreed with Worley that the

111

problem was not limited to Kress's and Woolworth's, but he concentrated on these two because he felt they were the "key to the situation," and that if they would integrate, "the others would fall into line."

Relations between the committee and C. L. Harris were not good, for Harris resented being singled out, and he continued to insist that if others would integrate he would also. He saw no reason why he should have to lead change. The meetings between the committee and Harris were apparently not without friction, and one report had Zane being "pretty rough" on the Woolworth's manager. At one point Zane threatened to have Woolworth's license to operate taken away by the City Council on the basis that Woolworth's method of operation was incompatible with the safety and well-being of the community. This was seriously considered, for Zane and Waldo Falkener both discussed it and did not bring it before the City Council only because they were not certain they had enough votes. Harris continually pointed to the other stores, and Zane would reply, "I'm not interested in what the others do. It's up to you." Other committee members described Harris as "the fly in the ointment," and said, "He was going to hell before he'd integrate."

Zane's pressure on Harris was not successful. As Zane described one meeting: "Yesterday evening, I held a meeting with operators of lunch counters in variety stores and after two hours and fifteen minutes of discussion, I was unable to break down their adamant stand against any form of change in present policy." He went on to say that the stores appeared to be concerned only with economic factors.

More meetings were held, and the committee conferred with the Woolworth area manager in Atlanta. "We understand that the area manager in Atlanta was expressing the attitude of the New York office in declining the committee recommendation." The committee did not confer with the Kress headquarters, but Zane was quoted as saying that he felt the opposition of the local manager, H. E. Hogate, was sufficient to cause rejection of the proposals.

On March 31, Zane met with the student leaders at the Hayes-Taylor YMCA to tell them negotiations had failed. He told the students, however, that he did not feel the time had been wasted. The students agreed. In a letter Zane wrote later, he said: "They [the students] said they believed they understood the problem better. They, and many others, gave thought to it when I don't believe they would have done so if the committee had not been formed."

The relations between the committee and the students were extremely good during this whole period, and much of this was due to Ed Zane's work. There was confidence on the part of the students that the committee was sincere, and each group trusted the other. Some of the individual committee members' feelings about the students were mixed —one member felt there was a certain amount of "impudence" in the students, and another characterized Ezell Blair Jr. as a "nut"—but the majority of the committee and most people who came in contact with the students were impressed. Two of them, Mayor Roach and Slim Kendall of the *Daily News*, were tremendously impressed with the students' seriousness and earnestness.

Even at A & T, the administration was very pleased with the way the students handled themselves. President Gibbs felt that many grew up during this period, and Dean Gamble had only two major cases of discipline during the sit-ins. In the first week one boy was arrested for being drunk and carrying a knife; he was expelled. Later during the picketing one of the student leaders was roughed up

113

and a group of thirty to forty A & T students started for the business section to "get" somebody. Dean Gamble heard about it, and he was able to catch up with them before they reached the downtown area and persuade them to return to the campus.

Ed Zane, who dealt more directly with the students than anyone else in the white community, was never disappointed in them and the Negro community felt the same way about him. In a personal letter to Zane, Waldo Falkener wrote, "Members of my race have been deeply impressed by your sincerity and understanding." Dr. Gibbs wrote him a letter during the period thanking him for his efforts, and Dean Gamble spoke of Zane as a "very fine and public-spirited person." Zane, on his part, in an office memo to Spencer Love, wrote, "Incidentally, the attitude of students, faculty, and business leaders of the colored community was exemplary and would have done credit to any group regardless of race."

The month of March saw statements on the sit-ins by the Governor of North Carolina, the President of the United States, and a former President. Governor Luther Hodges, in a prepared statement released on March 13, said he had no sympathy for sit-in demonstrators "who deliberately engage in activities which any reasonable person can see will result in a breakdown of law and order." He deplored what he said was "interference with the normal and proper operation of a private business." The statement did not mention the governor's part ownership of a Howard Johnson Restaurant between Chapel Hill and Durham in which demonstrations had occurred.

President Eisenhower was asked at a press conference whether he would call a White House conference to discuss the sit-ins. He replied that conferences aimed at settling racial tensions should be held in every Southern community, rather than nationally. "I am one of those persons that believes there is too much interference in the private affairs, and, you might say, personal lives already. And I would like to diminish rather than increase it." Asked specifically about the sit-ins, he replied that he would "reserve judgment on the sit-down disorders." As for restaurants he said the matter had been before the Supreme Court several times. He went on to say he was "not a lawyer," but it was his general understanding that when a restaurant operates under a public charter, "certainly all members of the public have equal rights." The Norfolk *Journal and Guide* said Eisenhower "missed another chance to go down in history as a truly great President." He was, the paper said, "passing the responsibility."

When former President Harry S Truman was asked *his* opinion, he replied, "If anyone came into my store and tried to stop business, I'd throw him out. The Negro should behave himself and show he's a good citizen." The NAACP wired Truman to find out if he had been misquoted, but he had not. "I would do just what I said I would. . . . I would say the same thing for all the newspapers and televisions in the country."

In March, a speech Chancellor Gordon Blackwell had made to Woman's College students on February 9 was made public:

> . . . Your responsibilities as students of Woman's College goes beyond personal considerations . . . On and off the campus you represent this institution.
>
> There is no blinking the fact that participation in this demonstration by several of our students, no matter how high their motives, definitely increased

115

the inflammatory qualities of the situation. . . .

I strongly urge each of you to weigh carefully the probable consequences of any action that you may contemplate. . . . More specifically I advise each of you to refrain from any public demonstration in connection with the issue now before the community or any similar issue which may arise in the future.

The speech caused a furor. One letter to the editor from a white minister strongly criticized Blackwell's stand: "The implication which the chancellor seems to draw is that a student ought never to think or act according to any personal conviction unless that conviction be in harmony with the 'official line.' What this position implies for freedom in education is quite frightening." Blackwell replied that his speech was not intended to deny the right of students to participate, and he was strongly defended in the *Daily News*. The morning paper termed the speech on "sound ground in urging students to refrain from participation in demonstrations which might lead to violence. Chancellor Blackwell's speech has been given the wrong twist; it was aimed not at interference with student freedom but with preserving the peace, keeping W.C. students out of danger, and aiding rapprochement which was sorely needed."

Outside of Greensboro, the list of cities that were experiencing sit-ins was growing. Charleston, Columbia, Miami, Houston, San Antonio, and even Xenia, Ohio, were added to the list, and by the end of the month sixty-eight cities in thirteen states had had some form of sit-in. There were interesting variations. At Petersburg, Virginia, and Memphis, Tennessee, students started sit-ins or read-ins at the local public libraries for whites, and at Elizabeth City, North Carolina, students who had been refused service at

116

the local lunch counter staged a picnic. Memphis had a sit-in at a local art gallery; some Southern churches had kneel-ins; and at Biloxi, Mississippi, in April, Negroes staged a wade-in at the white public beach in that city.

Planning for the sit-ins increased greatly as the young students gained experience. In Atlanta, when a lunch-counter manager called the police to get the students away from her counter, a harried police officer could only answer, "Lady, they're all over town. Just be patient and we'll get to you as fast as we can." Atlanta students ran a full-page ad in the local newspaper entitled "An Appeal for Human Rights," which Governor Ernest Vandiver dismissed as a "left-wing" document: "Obviously it was not written by students. . . . Nor, in fact, did it read like it was written even in this country."

At Columbia, South Carolina, a light-skinned Negro was served, but when he passed his hamburger over to a darker friend, the counter was immediately closed. The Governor of Tennessee charged that demonstrations in Nashville had been "instigated, planned by, and staged for the convenience of CBS," after television crews were on hand when students resumed sit-ins. Southern legislatures and city governments began working on laws that would prohibit the sit-ins, and arrests became more frequent. In Nashville, seventy-five students were jailed and refused bond; in Montgomery, Alabama, a sociology professor from Indiana and eleven of his students were jailed while making a study of a community during racial strife. On March 15 alone, some five hundred protesters were jailed across the South.

There was other news, however, and the political campaigns were beginning to go into full swing. Richard Nixon seemed to have the Republican nomination all but sewed up, while John F. Kennedy and Hubert H. Humphrey, the two announced candidates, were politicking and entering primaries all over the nation in an effort to gain the Democratic nomination. Later in the month Stuart Symington of Missouri would announce his candidacy, but Senate majority leader Lyndon B. Johnson had not yet, he said, decided whether to run. The Catholic issue was being hotly debated, and *Time* magazine commented in early March that "Jack Kennedy has the smoothest-running, widest-ranging, most efficient personal organization in the Democratic Party today." In California, two events caught the national attention. Dr. Bernard Finch and his girl friend Carole Tregoff were being tried for the murder of Finch's wife, and convicted murderer Caryl Chessman, making his ninth appeal on a death sentence scheduled to take place in May, caused Governor Pat Brown to call a special session of the California legislature to debate capital punishment.

But racial news still seemed to be the number-one story. In Congress the first civil-rights bill since Reconstruction was about to be passed, while in South Africa the world was shocked by the massacre of over seventy natives at Sharpsville. Newspapers editorialized warmly on both the civil-rights bill and Sharpsville, but to sixty-eight Southern cities their own racial problems seemed more important. In March the Greensboro *Daily News* wrote: "What happens in the U. S. Senate or what happens in South Africa may not be nearly so important as what happens in our community. We must somehow find a path through the current difficulty and a just and honorable pattern of behavior for all men and women of whatever race or creed, inexorably bound up in the crisis of commerce and conscience."

118

Different Southern communities were finding different patterns of behavior, and these were not always just or honorable. In Montgomery, Alabama, a white man clubbed a demonstrating Negro woman with a baseball bat. The Montgomery *Advertiser* urged arrest of the white man and carried a photo of him with his name. The man was well known to the local police but no arrest was ever made. In Tallahassee, tear gas was used to break up a march, and at Bessemer, Alabama, a white man beat Negroes with iron pipes. At Orangeburg, South Carolina, in 40-degree weather, firemen and police turned high-powered hoses on marching students, sending several who had been hit squarely to the hospital. The 350 students, still wet, were then herded into an open stockade. The lieutenant governor of South Carolina, Burnett Maybank, commended "the cool, deliberate manner in which the incidents have been handled by our law enforcement officers."

Various colleges were also having their difficulties, and although the majority said simply and quite honestly that they could not control their students, some institutions felt obliged to do something. At Alabama State College, nine students were expelled, and shortly thereafter a thousand students started a boycott of classes. At Louisiana Southern University in Baton Rouge, after eighteen leaders had been expelled, school leaders—fearing the reaction of state officials—had to plead with four thousand students not to carry out the threat of a mass walkout.

At Vanderbilt University, a Negro theology student in the divinity school, Reverend James M. Lawson, who had been to India and was instructing Fisk University students in nonviolent passive resistance techniques, was asked to resign from the school three months before his scheduled graduation. The action, without precedent at Vanderbilt,

119

was taken by the executive committee of the Board of Trustees, and followed no unusual procedure for expulsion. The Nashville sit-ins had begun on February 29, and on March 1 the Nashville *Banner* ran an editorial on Lawson in which it said he was "out-Kaspering Kasper," equating Lawson and the white segregationist who a few years earlier had stirred white Tennesseans to decidedly nonpassive techniques of avoiding school integration. The publisher of the *Banner* was on the executive committee, as were several local merchants, and three days later this group voted to expel Lawson. Divinity students held a mass meeting protesting the "grave error" of the university, and the faculty protested. At a dedication of the new divinity school quadrangle that month, guest speakers publicly criticized the school's position. Dean Liston Pope of Yale Divinity School said, "My presence here today is by no means to be construed as an endorsement of the recent action of the university. . . . Only the expression of opposition by students and faculty of the school has served to preserve its reputation among sister institutions." But Lawson was not readmitted, and Vanderbilt's troubles were not over.

Still, some progress was being made. In most communities interracial committees were being formed to discuss the problem, and in Salisbury and Winston-Salem, North Carolina, on March 7, several drug stores served Negroes at lunch counters, breaking the color line for the first time. San Antonio's variety stores integrated their lunch counters successfully, and at Lenoir, North Carolina, when six Negro students came in to use the "white" public library, they were not asked to leave.

Public officials also began backing the students. In Atlanta, Mayor William B. Hartsfield said in response to

120

the demonstrations and their critics, "Some of the things expressed . . . are, after all, the legitimate aspirations of young people throughout the nation and the entire world." And in Florida Governor Leroy Collins went on statewide television and attacked some of the actions taken toward the students, giving what amounted to an informal sermon on the moral indefensibility of lunch-counter segregation. "The city of Tallahassee took a rather rigid and punitive position . . . and we finally developed conditions in Tallahassee of which I am frankly ashamed. . . . I think that it is unfair and morally wrong to single out one department though and say he [the merchant] does not want or will not allow Negroes to patronize that one department. Now he has the legal right to do that, but I still don't think that he can square that right with moral, simple justice."

When Ed Zane met with the mayor on April 1, the press noted obvious fatigue in Zane's speech and actions. He had worked for over a month to find a solution to Greensboro's most serious problem, and he had not been successful. More than a week before the meeting with the mayor he knew his efforts would not succeed, and he was fearful of the consequences of that failure. As he wrote to Spencer Love on March 25, "Realizing the explosive potential of the situation and what will take place once that information is made public, I dread to even think about the consequences to the general community welfare."

In his statement to the mayor, Zane gave an account of the committee's activities. He pointed out that the committee had no legal power to force action: "Your committee, realizing that it has no authority and can be of help only in an advisory capacity, set out to confer with representatives of the Negro race, the operators of businesses

121

that serve food . . . and with citizens." In pointing to the failure of the variety stores to accept the committee's recommendation of partial integration, Zane gave this reason:

> The managers are extremely sensitive to public reaction, and merchants engaged in general merchandising businesses who also have food departments are fearful that if they serve all races on an integrated basis in the food department, they will lose a sufficient percentage of their present patronage to the nonintegrated eating establishments in our city to cause a presently profitable food department to operate at a loss.

Mayor Roach also issued a statement: "I am calling on the management of the stores to place the safety and good of this community above their own personal desires and to operate these business establishments in such a manner as to eliminate racial tensions."

In the weeks since Ed Zane had first been to see him, Mayor Roach had begun to take a much more active part in attempts at settlement. He wired the national presidents of Woolworth's and Kress's asking them to open the counters. He also asked the mayors of Durham and Charlotte to meet to discuss the problem, but neither was interested. Mayor Roach was not on the committee, but, sometimes accompanied by General Townsend, the city manager, he would make personal visits to the store managers and leading Negroes. He described Mr. Harris as being "noncooperative as he could be," and as the weeks progressed, found himself more and more on the side of the students—and making ever more forceful statements. Dr. Gibbs of A & T is one who feels that Mayor Roach played a large part in building a constructive atmosphere in Greensboro. On nu-

122

merous occasions the mayor went to talk with Gibbs, and Gibbs says he appreciated the work done by Roach much more after noticing the actions of other mayors.

The Southern Regional Council wrote that "one of the more heartening occurrences of the past two months has been the temperate and affirmative stand of a number of Southern mayors." George Roach was one of these mayors.

7

The Stalemate

*I'm going to let you in, but
I want to let you know that you
will be arrested for trespass.*

AT WOOLWORTH's on April 1, C. L. Harris was asked
by the press what he planned to do in the light of the
committee report. Harris replied, "I'm not going to do anything." He pointed out once again that he "resented being
singled out from other food merchants," and that his store
was "not any different from establishments that sell food
only." The Mayor's Committee had no plans for any meeting in the future, for it knew of nothing else it could do.
At the variety stores, white toughs were again heckling
the Negro students, and it was apparent that the situation
was little changed from the first week in February except
that it was perhaps less spectacular.

On Saturday, April 2, the Greensboro *Daily News*
headlined, "Two Stores Blamed by Committee." The story
mentioned only Woolworth's and Kress's, which brought a
quick reply from Zane and Worley. In the next morning's
paper, a story headlined "Two Mayor's Committee Members Dcny Placing Blame on Stores" reported that the two
men felt Woolworth's and Kress's had been done an injustice by the *Daily News* story. The committee, they said,
had met with representatives of twelve eating establish-

ments, none of which had agreed to integrate. Worley made this statement: "At no time did any member of the committee express the opinion that they were at fault. The premise on which all our meetings were held was that a merchant has a right to operate his business as he sees fit." Apparently Woolworth's found the story unfair, for their attorneys were sent to the *Daily News* office to discuss the matter.

But when Mayor Roach was questioned by newsmen about the story and its emphasis on the two stores, he said, "I am addressing the management of Kress and Woolworth," he said. "They're the only stores where there's been trouble."

In the April 1 report, the committee had said that the students agreed to go along with partial integration of the lunch counters, but the merchants had not accepted. On the following day, this was refuted by Ezell Blair Jr.: "We just talked about it. We never accepted anything like that." The students wanted complete integration of the lunch counters. On Sunday, April 3, Thurgood Marshall spoke at Bennett against the committee's suggestion of "token integration."

Following the statement of failure by the Mayor's Committee, the Student Executive Committee for Justice also released a statement:

Despite public sentiment for removal of racial barriers at lunch counters, despite the countless hours spent by the Mayor's Committee to arrive at an acceptable solution, and despite the principle involved, the variety stores are still reluctant to correct the existing situation.

. . . it seems entirely inconceivable to us that the very same persons who have utilized the principle

126

of democracy in establishing for themselves a multi-million dollar livelihood should turn the tables and take away from others the rights to which they are entitled under these very same principles. They are willing to reap the harvest but they are unwilling to plant the seeds.

The students' committee went on to ask for continued support by the people of Greensboro "who have already demonstrated widespread confidence in our cause."

On April 2, the counters shut down. Harris said his closing was ordered by C. M. Purdy, head of the Woolworth regional office. H. E. Hogate at Kress's said he had not received similar instructions from his company but when the picketers attempted to take seats, he closed the counter. Outside, a line of students marched back and forth in front of the stores.

As the weeks passed, the situation remained the same. Every day four or five students picketed each store. Usually two white girls who were students at Bennett were among the pickets, occasionally joined by a few Woman's College girls. The signs for the picketers reportedly were made at Woman's College by one of the girls who had participated in the first week's sit-in.

At Woolworth's the counter remained closed "until such time as a satisfactory solution can be reached," but one source close to Harris said the Woolworth manager was ready to issue trespass warrants should the counter open and the students resume sit-ins. Kress's reopened its counter on April 6, and at first only a few students sat at the counter each day. But on April 11, when thirty-four demonstrators sat down, Hogate closed the counter. Thirty minutes after the students left, he reopened it. The students returned, and he was forced to close again.

127

For the next few days, Hogate followed a similar course, keeping the counter open until a student appeared and then closing it. One student who seemed to be in charge—Roland Hanna, who for some reason called himself "Mr. X"—jumped on the Kress's counter several times. On April 15, Kress's installed a chain around the counter and started using the "host" method for letting in white customers. The students were informed that they would be arrested if they did enter. None did.

With the initiating of pickets in April, the Negro students were joined by counterpickets, among them the boys who had staged the counter-sit-ins in February. Many of these had police records. The white counterpickets were there every day the Negro pickets were present, and on one occasion two of the whites picketed City Hall in a prosegregation demonstration. Their signs, usually hastily made with a felt marking pen on big sheets of poster paper, carried slogans like "Nigger what do you want? the whole world?" "Go Back to Cotton Fields Nigger," "Don't want you, Don't need you, Go Home Nigger," and other assorted phrases. One of the more practical signs suggested, "Build your own cafe Nigger," and another in a bow to subtlety bore the single word "Nigger."

There were several incidents, but no violence. One boy was arrested for throwing a stinkbomb, and the police had to ask a nearby novelty store owner not to sell the bombs while the picketing was going on. The owner consented. When the police told one white boy to move along, his answer showed a practical knowledge of the law along with a certain fatalism: "You can't do anything to me for walking. It's my right as much as theirs. If one of them gets in my way, I'll lay him through the Kress window or put him out in the center line in the street. It's simple assault. I

128

The sit-in at Woolworth's before the lunch counter shut down in April, 1960. *Photo: Greensboro News Record.*

can't get but thirty days. What's thirty days? I might live sixty-five years." Another boy was wearing a chain as a belt around his waist. A driver passed by and shouted, "What are you going to do with that chain?" "I'm going to wrap it around some nigger's head in a minute," was the answer. The police made him remove the chain. Klansmen were present, and it was reported that the youths who picketed were paid by the Klan.

Kluds, Klagles, Klaverns, and Klans—image of the Klan. It is the specter of the rednecked, vapid-eyed, illiterate man—a man lynching, hating, bombing, burning—a picture of men in coveralls, brogans, and old felt hats dressing up in sheets, costumes of another century. Last of the clay-eaters, they say, the ignorant, the rabble, the unredeemed with their Grand Dragons, burning crosses, mystic rites, men yelling "Nigger, go home," "Back to Africa, nigger," "Nigger, nigger, nigger." Image of the Klan.

On a rainy morning, George Dorsett comes up in a London Fog raincoat. He is wearing a tastefully tailored sports coat, conservative tie, a small diamond ring, gold cuff links, and well-polished shoes of expensive leather. There is nothing special about the day—just a Saturday on which he has come uptown to have a cup of coffee and do some shopping. He might be any successful local businessman, except that there is no mass-produced look about George Dorsett. He is of medium height and well-built, with strong, handsome features and thick black wavy hair, which he combs straight back. He looks to be in his midforties, but is probably five to ten years older. Meeting him, there would be no way to tell that he is a member of the Klan, unless you noticed the small red triangular pin he

130

wears in his lapel, a pin that might be that of a Rotarian, Kiwanian, or Civitan. It isn't: this pin has three small letters on it, all of them *K*.

George Dorsett is a quiet, easy man, obviously sure of himself. He is a persuasive talker—he does not rant or rave —and although he will make an occasional grammatical error, he thinks over what he says, never slipping off into the kind of rhetoric one might expect. He feels that the press and police have been fair, although he disagrees with certain editorial policies and is sure that the police have misquoted some laws to Klan members to get them off the street. Among strangers he will usually refer to Negroes as "the colored race."

He is also very careful in what he does. Police say frankly that he never gets caught at anything. In 1960 he was present at the sit-ins almost every day, but invariably as a bystander, simply observing. He did participate in the counter-sit-in movement, but generally by standing away, conferring with his men, giving advice, or just observing. During the picketing he would drive by and confer with some of the marchers, but he never took a direct part. When asked what he meant when he said, "I am here to keep violence to a minimum," he has answered that he didn't remember making the statement, but that he was probably misquoted. He would have tried to prevent violence, he has said, not keep it to a minimum. He has also recounted the incident in which two truck drivers who had been drinking came in the side entrance of Woolworth's with the intention of assaulting some students. Dorsett was there and was able to talk them out of it.

He was chaplain of the state Klan in 1960, and some observers felt he was the most powerful Klan figure in the state. His correct title is Reverend; he is a Baptist minister.

131

He helped found the Southside Baptist Church in Greensboro and was its original pastor, and has had other congregations in the Greensboro area. Dorsett is an effective evangelist—he has held revivals in Texas and other Southern states—and with his swept-back hair, his intense eyes, good looks, and a little of the accent of the North Carolina hills, there is much that suggests Billy Graham. His voice has a certain scratchiness which results from strain at revivals, but he is a powerful speaker, and this training as an evangelist has undoubtedly been helpful to him in his Klan work.

The Reverend George Dorsett. *Photo: Greensboro Daily News.*

Many of Dorsett's preacher friends ask him how he can reconcile his position with Christianity. He says he has asked himself this question, whether he is doing the right thing, and he believes he is. He knows his Bible and says, "the enemy has attacked." He points out that God is not the author of confusion, and that the civil rights groups have stirred up all this confusion.

In 1957 a Greensboro unit of the Klan was formed, and Dorsett joined that year. He says that he has just always been a "diehard" against desegregation. He quickly became active in Klan affairs, and was present at the unfortunate— for the Klan—Maxton, North Carolina, rally in 1958. That night the local Lumbee Indians decided to take matters into their own hands. In effect, they went on the warpath, driving the Klan away from the rally and virtually out of the state. According to Dorsett (he is not allowed to give membership figures), membership went down and things slowed up after that affair. Then came the 1960 variety-store sit-ins.

Dorsett first went to Woolworth's on February 3, but he was aware of the sit-ins early the day before. He has said his sources included members of the colored community and of the police department, and there is little reason to doubt him. He simply knows too much. He is aware that Ralph Johns was instrumental in starting the movement, and he knows the names of many of the people who were behind the scenes. Dorsett was born in St. Louis, but he has lived in Greensboro since he was seven and he knows many people there. Part of his success in the Klan can be traced to his acquaintances and sources throughout the city.

George Dorsett has denied that the Klan paid the boys to picket. He points out that eighteen is the minimum age for Klan members, and that few in the organization are

The Reverend George Dorsett. *Photo: Greensboro Daily News.*

under twenty-one; also, there would be little point in paying high school students if Klansmen were present. Dorsett feels the Klan is unjustly blamed for many things that happened. He says the Klan will "sometimes use pressure," but he denies the use of late-night telephone calls and hate letters. "We try to stay away from intimidation and threats." Dorsett points out that telephone calls can be traced and that use of the mails for such purposes is a federal offense. He says the Klan tries to work through business concerns, using financial pressure. "Hit them in the pocketbook," he has said.

But fairly or not, the rumors persisted that the Klan was behind all the trouble as letters and phone calls continued to be a problem. For Ed Zane it was the telephone calls, the threats of bombing. "I never knew when I stepped on my gas pedal if the car would blow up." He reported all calls and letters to the FBI, but the threats continued. He was told that acid would be thrown in his wife's face— that he would never be able to recognize her again—and that his grandchildren were in danger. Mayor Roach also was threatened; his wife called him up at work, crying, and told him that she had just received a list of the ten Greensboro men who would be killed, including him. And for most of the committee, there were the letters: "Why don't you nigger-loving trash parade with niggers! Let the people see who are supporting them—why hide? We know you committee members are two-faced uncouth bastards trying to force niggers on whites to raise your social standing. We are watching your every move for retaliation soon—when we strike may the Lord keep you."

But most of these people have said the letters and the crank calls really didn't bother them. "The ones you fear are those who don't write or call," one pointed out. Ed

135

Zane said, "I'm a Southerner, I knew I'd get them," and he tried not to let them bother him. But something did bother Zane, and that was the reaction of some of his friends. Some turned against him and a few would not speak to him because of his participation on the committee.

On April 11, the activities of the students widened as they expanded their protest to local shopping centers and other establishments that served Negroes at merchandise counters but not at lunch counters. At a number of places they were served standing up, but most counters closed when the Negroes took seats. At the Friendly Shopping Center the students picketed Eckerd's Drug Store, but when told the shopping center was on private property and they would be arrested if they did not leave, they left.

At the Summit Shopping Center, they picketed a drug store and a dairy bar. Here they were also told they were on private property, but Oscar Burnett, owner of the center, told them he would meet with them to discuss the problem. Burnett, a successful businessman, had been very much interested in the sit-ins, and he had offered Ed Zane his help and several suggestions. "This is a practical approach," he told Zane, "and does not involve brotherly love, which I hope and pray will come in time all over the world." When he met with the students that night, he told them he could do nothing about the policies of the drug store and dairy bar, and legally he could have them arrested. But he would allow picketing if they agreed to limit the number of pickets to two. He would supply private police protection for the picketers. The students, although they wanted more pickets, agreed to his conditions.

It was during these first weeks in April that the strategy of the Negroes and their demands for equal service took a significant turn with a boycott of the two stores. A boycott had been going on for some weeks in Nashville, where a

136

merchant was quoted as saying, "This thing has frightening ramifications. It is more serious than most people realize. It has now become an economic situation affecting the entire community." The Negroes realized they had a powerful weapon, and the CORE boycott coordinator reported that Woolworth's national business had dropped 8.9 percent in the month of March.

On April 12, in Greensboro, Dr. George Simkins publicly urged Negroes to stay "away from stores where they have lunch-counter facilities and refuse to serve Negroes," but this had been going on for some time before. On April 9, students were seen in the two stores urging other Negroes not to buy. A manager who saw them accused the students of bad faith, starting a boycott while negotiations were going on.

It was apparent, however, that negotiations weren't going on. The Mayor's Committee had not met for several weeks, and other efforts at settlement had also failed. George Trosper, Executive Vice President of the Merchants Association, had tried to arrange a meeting between the leaders of the Student Executive Committee and the merchants, but he was unable to raise a quorum. Most of the merchants felt they were not under fire, and they did not want to get involved.

The students had hoped by picketing to arouse public opinion and thus force a change on the part of the variety stores. But public opinion was not aroused, and as the daily demonstrations continued, less and less newspaper space, editorials, and letters to the editor resulted. Greensboro still seemed unconcerned, and public opinion appeared, in fact, to be turning against the students. In a survey taken by Belmont Abbey College on April 9 and 10, white people who said they were customers of the variety stores were asked whether they would continue to patronize lunch counters if Negroes were served. Only 30 percent of some 1,330 questioned said yes. This seemed to confirm Mr. Harris's belief that the people who wanted his store integrated never shopped there. Other surveys showed there had been no great change in feeling on the question of integration. The same poll was taken by Belmont Abbey students in Charlotte, where 58 percent said they would not patronize the counter.

On the weekend of April 16, a three-day meeting was held at Shaw University in Raleigh to try to coordinate the goals and tactics of the sit-ins. Students from Negro colleges all over the South attended, along with many white students from both the North and the South. A & T students, among them Ezell Blair, were present. Numerous subcommittee meetings were held to discuss the different problems, and Reverend James Lawson, the expelled Vanderbilt divinity student, spoke to the students.

But the keynote address was given by Dr. Martin Luther King Jr. "The demand," he said, "is not simply for service at a lunch counter. . . . It is a demand for respect." He concluded with advice to the students, three practical suggestions: they should form permanent organizations so that when the school term ended the protest would continue; they should start selective buying campaigns in their communities; and they should be prepared to go to jail and not accept bond.

The Greensboro students were listening. On April 21, they entered Kress's, went to the lunch counter, and took seats. Forty-five were arrested.

The students had arrived at about 12:30 that afternoon and had stood in front of the chained entrance to the luncheonette. They were quiet and orderly. There appeared to be some argument among them as to the course

138

of action, but they remained standing at the entrance. At about 1 P.M., the fire chief arrived and advised them of fire regulations, saying they were blocking an entrance and would have to move. The students left. At 1:30 a student called aside a detective who was present and asked whether it would be trespassing if they entered the lunch-counter area. The detective told the student it was trespassing in any manner if the manager had so stated.

The student left, but at about 2 P.M. the whole body of students returned and entered the lunch-counter area to take seats. Hogate, the manager, held the chain open for them, saying, "I'm going to let you in, but I want to let you know that you will be arrested for trespass." The students did not move. At 2:15 the police started arresting students. A few left, but the majority remained and forty-five were taken in. Among those arrested were Ezell Blair Jr., Joseph McNeil, David Richmond, and the two white girls from Bennett. Dr. George Simkins, who had been present the whole time, went to the police station to supply bail, but the students were released without bail.

The Greensboro *Champion,* a Negro newspaper, praised the students in a page-one editorial by Ralph Johns under his pen name Ricardo Raffles:

> On last Thursday, the valiant sit-down warriors of Greensboro joined the immortal ranks of those martyrs who are being jailed all over the South while increasing their right of equal, just and equitable treatment in places of public accommodation. . . . For the sacrifices being made by our young people today will make our country a better place tomorrow.

Every week in the *Champion* Johns wrote one of his torrid editorials, but for a man who wanted to take part,

139

who had helped start the whole thing, writing was a poor substitute. But Johns could do no more, and in truth his usefulness to the movement had ended when the boys first took a seat at the counter on February 1. For ten years Johns had been urging, pushing, imploring the local Negroes to do something, but when they did, he could do little else. The students still came by his store after each day's demonstration, but it was more out of respect than for guidance: they knew what they were doing. He advised the students to court arrest, but he was realistic enough to know that if he were a part of it the movement would be discredited.

Johns attempted to exert some pressure in the white community, and he went to see Mayor Roach and Ed Zane, but these men would have little to do with him—you do not waste your time with crackpots. In the Negro community he also had little influence, many were unaware of the role he had played. At one meeting of Negro leaders, Johns was the only white man present; when he attempted to speak one of the Negro ministers, who had only belatedly given the students support, told him that no outside help was needed. This was a Negro movement. George Simkins quickly stood up and defended Johns, and the minister apologized. The majority of the Negro community, if they did not know his part in the sit-ins, did know what he had done over the years, and they respected Johns.

By this time Johns saw the support the sit-ins were getting, and he no longer desired anonymity. In a telegram to Roy Wilkins, Executive Secretary of the NAACP, the *Champion* urged the NAACP to award the Spingarn Medal, an annual award to the person who has done the most to fight discrimination in America, to the four boys and "to the white Greensboro merchant who inspired the movement

140

and gave initial financial support." But the award went to neither the boys nor the merchant; Johns's role remained largely anonymous.

The police had known the students were going to risk arrest—the previous day a Negro had phoned a detective assigned to the demonstrations to advise him that most of the students wanted to go into Kress's on the twenty-first, and to ask about bond and arrest. The building of communications between the police and the students was slow: in the initial sit-ins and during the later picketing, the students came to expect complete fairness from the police, and because they knew that they both needed and could get police protection, communications gradually developed.

The only instance of bad faith was on the part of the students. A few days before the arrests at Kress's, one of the student leaders advised the police that Negroes were going to come in and attempt to be arrested at Kress's the next day. The police were on hand in full force, prepared for any trouble, but the students did not come that day. When the boy who had talked to them was questioned, he replied that it was a hoax to keep the police on their toes. The policemen gave the student a long lecture on the ethics of dealing with police officers. This kind of thing never happened again, and relations between the two groups remained smooth.

The press praised the actions of the Greensboro police. The Raleigh *Times,* commenting after the first week of demonstrations in Greensboro, said: "North Carolina can be grateful—and thankful to the Greensboro police—for the fact that there was no real trouble during the time the sitdown strike was actually going on. . . . Greensboro police were on hand to keep order, and they did keep order." The Greensboro *Record* editorialized on February 10, "Greensboro has a Police Department of which to be proud. We think of the admirable way in which it dealt with the emergency situation created by the Negro students' sit-downs." The Negro press also joined in. The Norfolk *Journal and Guide* commented: "One thing which it pleases us very much to say: The police officers covering the demonstrations conducted themselves very becomingly . . . whether it was in Greensboro or Norfolk, that much can be said."

Mayor Roach was probably closer to the police at this time than any other city official, and he felt they performed a "Herculean task in handling the situation." Roach has talked about the excellence of Police Chief Paul Calhoun—not as the mayor, but as an individual citizen who was truly impressed by the force.

Police Chief Paul B. Calhoun is a friendly, medium-sized man with graying and slightly disheveled hair, and rapid-fire speech that is unusual in a native North Carolinian. He is not a particularly imposing man, and if it were not for the uniform and pistol which he wears at all times, it would be difficult to imagine him as a police officer. He certainly does not fit the hard-bitten stereotype. But there is little doubt that Calhoun is a man who is proud of being a policeman and proud of his force. For almost thirty years he has been on the Greensboro police force, since 1956 as its chief, and he will say quite frankly that the Greensboro force is unquestionably the best police department in the Southeast United States. If he hesitates as he makes this statement, one feels it is not because such a large area is mentioned but perhaps because more of the nation should have been included.

Before Calhoun became chief, he was in charge of the

142

police training program, and he feels that this program is one of the reasons the police force is so outstanding. He set up the formal continuing training fifteen years ago, and there are rigid regulations for becoming a police officer. "It's hard to get in, but easy to get out," he will say. The department has the usual physical regulations, but it also requires a high school diploma and the candidate must take a series of psychological tests. Of those who apply, only 7 percent make it, and those who do must go through a one-year probationary period. One result of all this is a feeling of pride among the men on the force. Greensboro police are generally respected by all segments of the community, and although there is strong discipline, the morale among the men is good.

The 1960 sit-ins being for the police, as for the entire community, something entirely new, they had no precedent to guide them. No one knew exactly what would happen, and Chief Calhoun has said the force simply followed the Boy Scout motto, "Be prepared." They had had some experience in dealing with other crowd situations, notably in labor disputes, and they tried to adapt this knowledge to the sit-in problem. The plainclothes officers, generally the more seasoned, were usually on duty inside the stores, while the uniformed police stayed outside to control the crowds and keep traffic moving. There was radio communication between the two stores, and if known troublemakers were spotted in the crowds, uniformed officers were assigned to stay near them as long as they were near the stores.

When the picketing began, juveniles were among those causing trouble. One of the most active detectives during this period was Captain William Jackson, then a lieutenant on the juvenile squad. In dealing with the counterpickets, Jackson would walk alongside the offender. As they walked,

143

Jackson would start talking quietly to the boy: "All right, son, when we reach the end of this store you're going to keep on walking straight ahead and turn that corner and there is going to be a police car and you're going to get in that car and come down to the station with me." The boys almost always did what Jackson said.

Chief Calhoun rarely went down to the variety stores during this period. The communications system made this unnecessary, and Calhoun felt strongly that it was important to have someone at the top to call the shots; he had "competent field commanders" to handle the situation. Once or twice he went to talk with C. L. Harris at Woolworth's and advise him on exactly what the police could do, but more often Harris came to talk to Calhoun at the police station—and he did not want it to appear that he was doing more than advising Harris on police matters.

But Calhoun's philosophy of the duties of a police chief goes beyond running an effective and efficient police force. He recognizes the limitations of the police officer and the bounds within which he must work. If asked, for instance, why he did not simply have his officer ask the four boys to move on that first day (there is a good possibility that the boys would have obeyed a policeman), Calhoun would answer firmly, "I don't have the right to ask them to move."

He also felt he had definite responsibilities to the community. One is the right of the public to know what is going on. His office was always open so that city officials, councilmen, the city manager, reporters, and others could get in touch with him or one of his top aides to find out exactly what was going on. The city officials were uniform in their praise of Calhoun in the handling of the different crises, and the press, usually the most critical of observers, praised the job Calhoun did. As one local newsman put

144

it, "Calhoun is a square fellow. He doesn't try to hide anything from you." Of course, the press at times printed things that Calhoun did not approve of, but he recognized and respected the fact that newspapermen are sensitive on the subject of their freedom of action. The Greensboro press and communications media were generally responsible, and, more important, reporters with their own sources could tip the police off on exclusive information they had received.

8

The Effects

*What are you gonna do about
all them chillun that got hosed?*

THE PICKETING continued. The students did not try to be arrested again, and every day a few would walk back and forth in front of the two variety stores. At the end of April the Civil Rights Act was passed, but this concerned voting rights, and the students' grievances at the lunch counters were not solved. May came, and across the nation the campaigns for the presidential nominations were picking up speed. John F. Kennedy, who won a surprise victory in West Virginia, appeared to be the front runner for the Democratic nomination. In North Carolina a gubernatorial campaign was in progress, and the segregationist candidate, Dr. I. Beverly Lake, was trying to pin the NAACP label on his opponents. Candidate Terry Sanford replied that he knew of no candidate "who would seek or want or accept any approval by the NAACP," and John Larkins, another hopeful, hitting back at Lake, contended that the NAACP "wants a hot-blooded segregationist candidate who will foment racial strife."

There was news other than civil rights and elections. On May 1, an American pilot, Francis Gary Powers, was shot down while flying over Russia. The State Department claimed he was flying a weather-reconnaissance mission, while the White House said the flight had been made without its knowledge. But there was little doubt that the U-2 was a U.S. spy plane, and the resulting furor wrecked the Summit Conference held in Paris that month. The payola scandals continued—Dick Clark saw nothing unusual about receiving over $400,000 in gifts and record royalties—and in California Caryl Chessman was put to death in the gas chamber. England's Princess Margaret married a commoner in May, while in Argentina Adolf Eichmann was kidnapped by Israeli agents.

Greensboro had its own excitement when in a public speech a local stockbroker blasted the Quakers, the original settlers in Guilford County, for being "un-American." The resulting outrage among Greensboro citizens resulted in almost as many letters to the editor as had the sit-ins. One of the biggest incidents that month concerned the flying of a Confederate flag. Out at Memorial Stadium, the general manager (a New Yorker) of the local baseball team had placed a Confederate flag on one of the flagpoles. Councilman Waldo Falkener argued that it was not appropriate to have a Confederate flag at the stadium, a memorial to the dead of World War I, and the flag was removed, but Falkener received hate calls over the incident.

There was still some news concerning the sit-ins. In Durham a fight involving fifteen to twenty people erupted at a Walgreen's Drug Store, and one Negro suffered a concussion. In Greensboro, by the second week in May, C. L. Harris announced he was reopening his counter; at Kress's, H. E. Hogate asked to be transferred. The Greensboro *Champion* ran a tremendous streamer on May 14, "Kress Manager Transferred," and "Ricardo Raffles" wrote, "It is bigots like the manager of the S. H. Kress here in Greensboro who . . . retard the cause of justice in our city. . . ."

Unfortunately for Hogate, he was transferred to Albany, Georgia, where in the following year Greensboro's racial troubles would seem minor in comparison.

In Winston-Salem on May 25, the lunch counters integrated, and the *Champion* headlined, "Winston Taste Good Like a Free Lunch Counter Should." A few other stores in such cities as Nashville and San Antonio had also integrated, but in Nashville the troubles surrounding Reverend James Lawson and Vanderbilt University continued. In April the Board of Trust of Vanderbilt had agreed to reconsider the Lawson case, but when it came up in May they refused to reverse the ruling of the executive committee. The divinity school faculty, expecting Lawson to be readmitted, was stunned, and one day after commencement the dean of the divinity school and eleven of the fifteen faculty members resigned. Thirteen other students left the school and three returned their diplomas, and all the Negro students at Vanderbilt withdrew. It was becoming evident that some members of the Board of Trust would simply let the divinity school disband, but when twenty-five other faculty members threatened resignation and even more expressed strong disapproval, the Chancellor of the school reversed his position and offered Lawson his degree based on transferred credits from Boston University, which he was attending at the time. Most of the faculty returned, but the dean of the divinity school was not asked back, and there was an attempt to shift the blame for the Lawson affair on him.

At the A & T commencement Dr. Frank Graham, former president of the University of North Carolina and a former United States Senator until his defeat in the racist campaign of 1950, told the students, "It is a matter of pride to me that this newest youth movement in our land had its

149

origin not in Moscow, but in North Carolina." But if the movement had originated in North Carolina, nothing had visibly changed in that state. The newspapers no longer carried stories on the demonstrations, and most students were preparing for exams or commencements. Across the South, the situation was similar. Students continued to demonstrate, but apparently the South was holding firm, and the movement that had started four months earlier at the Woolworth's lunch counter and had spread to practically every Negro college seemed actually to have accomplished very little.

But this was only a surface picture, and both white and Negro Southerners knew it. The change in attitudes and feelings among both races in the four months had been tremendous, and white Southerners, except for a few diehards, knew attitudes were not the only things that were going to change. Even the white boys who protested against the Negroes seemed to know it, to judge by the change in one of the chants they yelled at the students—from "Two, four, six, eight—we ain't gonna integrate," to "Two, four, six, eight—we don't want to integrate." Woolworth's representatives knew it and would admit privately as early as April that integration of the counters was inevitable. They still maintained publicly that they had to keep the counters segregated because other merchants would not integrate along with them, but when P. H. Werner of the Atlanta office made such a statement in April, he also said, "My thinking is that there are so many areas of importance to both races that the simple matter of eating at a lunch counter is not a major objective or goal."

Many white Southerners were getting an entirely new picture of the Negro. Most had believed that the Negro was reasonably happy, that he knew his place, and this be-

150

lief had been reinforced by the Negroes they had known —the maids, the yardmen. In a speech at Bennett College in February, Dr. Frederick D. Patterson, former president of Tuskegee Institute and a director of the Phelps-Stokes Fund, had explained this contact: "Custom and traditional relationships between the races in the South have been such as to permit day-to-day impersonal contacts which are necessary for normal existence to be confused with contacts of a personal, social nature which do not occur unless mutually agreeable."

The Negro had been in large part silent, and whites had interpreted this to signify lack of interest in desegregation. But now young, energetic Negroes were speaking out, telling white Southerners their feelings on segregation, destroying all beliefs in Negro contentment with Southern society. In Charlotte one student leader was quoted early in that city's demonstrations: "We are not only entitled to service, but we want it." And in Atlanta the full-page advertisement run by the students read in part: "The time has come for the people of Atlanta and Georgia to take a good look at what is really happening in this country and to stop believing those who tell us that everything is fine and equal and that the Negro is happy and satisfied."

Some whites cried out that the sit-ins and demonstrations all resulted from the lack of communication between the races, but to this one student replied, "Most whites think communications have broken down just because they're getting a new message. We've known all along what they were thinking—now they're learning what we think. And it doesn't fit in with their pet myths."

As for the moderate Southerner who had accepted segregation because he did not see the injustice and humiliation or did not want to see it, the sit-ins made them con-

151

scious and would bring some to action. James McBride Dabbs, a former president of the Southern Regional Council, wrote in April 1960:

> I am sure that many a white Southerner has become aware only within the last month that Negroes are not served at the lunch counters of ten cent stores. . . . Very few people question long established customs; they live by them without being aware of a privilege he didn't realize he had, and he may begin to question his right to it.

And when these whites saw these young, intent Negroes and the groups that opposed them, many had second thoughts. In Raleigh, an elderly white woman of the old school saw the Negro students being turned away. "They have no business refusing such nice, polite young people," she said. And in the Richmond *News-Leader,* the spokesman for "massive resistance" a few years earlier, this editorial appeared:

> Many a Virginian must have felt a tinge of wry regret at the state of things as they are, in reading of Saturday's "sit-downs" by Negro students in Richmond stores. Here were the colored students in coats, white shirts, ties, and one of them was reading Goethe and one was taking notes from a biology text. And here, on the sidewalk outside, was a gang of white boys come to heckle, a ragtail rabble, slackjawed, black-jacketed, grinning fit to kill, and some of them, God save the mark, were waving the proud and honored flag of the southern states in the last war fought by gentlemen. Eheu! It gives one pause.

Greensboro, whose Interracial Council had been abandoned in 1958, was now forced to rethink its positions on racial issues, and new groups and organizations were beginning to discuss the questions. Many white ministers and others who had not bothered to think about the situation before were giving public support to the students and offering their help finding a solution. It was far from a unanimous group, but it was a beginning.

But if the change in the white community was great, perhaps the change among Negroes was greater. There were still some voices from the past, of course. In Charlotte, a Negro minister and newspaper publisher, Dr. J. S. Goss, condemned the sit-ins as "uncalled for, unnecessary, ill advised, and inexpedient," and a Negro newspaper publisher in Anderson, South Carolina, Davis Lee, wrote that the student movement ". . . offers a serious threat to the conservative, intelligent leadership of our race and threatens to wipe out all Negro business for the mere privilege or right to eat in a white place. . . ." Still, the majority of adult Negroes came to support the students.

The movement was that of youth, however, and across the South some fifty thousand Negro students, both college and high school, were sitting in, demonstrating, and picketing. In some cases adult Negroes advised, but there were few participating in the sit-ins, and the younger ones really didn't care whether adults were present. It was their movement. In Alabama, one student expressed Negro students' feelings about adult participation when she talked about the college administrators: "We never were seriously interested in the approval or disapproval of our school administration. We decided that they should stay out of the movement for their own good, that we would not pull them into our activities." These young Negroes saw that their par-

153

ents living under the Southern system of segregation had done little to change things outwardly, and they did not want to rear their children in the same atmosphere. As Thurgood Marshall of the NAACP Legal Defense and Education Fund put it, "The young people are impatient. . . . And if you mean, are the young people impatient with me, the answer is yes."

Most of the students realized that in the society in which their parents had been brought up, dissent would not have been tolerated. In those years to belong to an organization such as the NAACP, to talk to a white person in any manner other than as an inferior, were things that few Negroes could do. Being able to bring cases involving discrimination to court, even talking in organizations like the Commission on Interracial Cooperation and the Southern Regional Council, trying to improve Negro schools— these were major accomplishments which had helped pave the way for the opening of Southern society. They also opened the bulwark of segregation to frontal attack.

But now the students were impatient with attacking the "foothills of segregation," as one head of the Southern Regional Council had expressed the goal of his organization, and it was time for direct action. The parents had helped pave the way, but they had not achieved the final goal. It would take a special group to do that, and it is perhaps not surprising that it was this generation that chose to do something about segregation in the South. An observer of the Negro college scene has described the Negro student of the fifties as primarily "quiescent and nonchalant," interested more in social fraternities than in social problems. But this was a new generation whose students had defied mobs in Little Rock, had been shouted at in Clinton, had had eggs thrown on them in Greensboro, and

154

had been spat upon in Charlotte. This was a generation of Negroes that had shown its fiber in countless ways, desegregating elementary and secondary schools throughout the South against the opposition of mayors, police chiefs, governors, and entire states. It was a generation that was now in college. And if each Negro child had silently wondered what he would have done—if he had been one of the nine students who integrated Little Rock, if mobs of white people had shouted and spat upon him as he walked all alone into a strange building where he knew there would be no friendly faces—he now had a chance to find out, a chance to make up for any guilt he might have felt for accepting things as they were.

The four A & T freshmen had been twelve years old when the Supreme Court handed down the *Brown* decision, fifteen when Central High in Little Rock was integrated. These were things they had seen with their own eyes, and they made an impression. To Joe McNeil, it seemed "that people in Alabama, where they had the Montgomery bus boycott, were at least trying to do something about it. The people in Little Rock, with the trouble at Central High School, were trying to do something. And we weren't." But they did, and it opened the way for the mass of Negro youth to do something. No longer was civil rights limited to the courts and legislative halls. It became a personal thing to each individual Negro, a pursuit of a goal of human dignity and freedom.

There were cries of communism and outside agitators, but as one Atlanta leader put it, "It's not Karl Marx and Khrushchev inspiring these students, but Jim Crow and Jesus Christ." Another commentator wrote, "It has been said that the South gave the Negro his greatest weapon—Christianity—and he's using it for all it's worth." These

155

were Southern Negroes, Negroes who had been brought up in the tradition of the spiritual and the revival, and many looked on the sit-ins as a type of religious crusade. But it was more than a crusade, more than a revival. The highly respected *Christian Century* discussed this aspect of the Negro religion:

It has always been a mistake to assume that the Negro's contribution to the religious life of America is limited to his joyous exuberance. It is especially clear now that religion is for him as for no other people in our land a sustenance and a power, inwardly sustaining him as he breaks barriers and crosses frontiers. . . . It is not surprising that the spectacle of wronged men and women peacefully and even joyously sustained by spiritual strength unknown to nominal Christians terrifies some people.

Before the students entered the stores there were Bible readings, and it was during these early sit-ins that many of the freedom songs that came out of the demonstrations of the sixties first appeared. These were students with confidence in their cause, a confidence that was mirrored in Ezell Blair Jr.'s statement that first week: "With God on our side, who can be against us?" But if older Negroes had also felt that God was on their side, these young ones no longer wanted to wait for some day of Jubilee far off in the future. As one student said smiling, "I expect God to help the student movement, but meanwhile the students will help the hell out of God." The day of Jubilee was now.

The nonviolence of the sit-ins naturally invited comparisons with Gandhi, and most of the students were aware of who he was and had read about him. Ezell Blair Jr. told a reporter in one interview, "I've never forgotten a televi-

156

sion story I saw last year called the Pictorial Story of India." The young freshman was impressed by the manner in which the strength of Gandhi's passive resistance seemed to grow each time he was thrown in jail, but Blair had never read any of Gandhi's works. A white student traveling in the South at that time interviewed some of the students in Durham. "I rarely felt Gandhi present among these Negroes as a significant or potent symbol," he wrote. "It was the Montgomery bus boycott in early manhood that had been the decisive event." Perhaps the best explanation of the influence of Gandhi came from a Florida Negro student's reaction to the cry of outside agitators: "Sure we've been influenced by outsiders, outsiders like Thoreau and Gandhi. But our biggest influence has been inside— all these years of second-class citizenship stored up inside us."

These Negroes had been brought up in the South; they had gone to schools there and were now in Southern Negro colleges. Of the more than three thousand A & T students, some 79 percent were from North Carolina. And if a Southern legislator might wonder why, he could take much of the blame. In trying to improve schools so they would be both "separate and equal" in an effort to stave off the *Brown* decision, in doing more for Negro higher education than any other section in the country—all in an effort to preserve segregation—he had taught Negroes in these improved schools that they held a citizenship and rights that were equal to every other American's. They had learned about the Constitution, the Declaration of Independence, the Emancipation Proclamation, and they saw what they believed they had a right to and wanted it. And they had seen the slowness of the courts and the actions legislatures

157

could take to circumvent court decisions, and they no longer wanted to wait for these.

Northern Negroes also attended these colleges, but they rarely took part in the struggle. If most of the Southerners seemed committed to the cause, it was the girls who supplied the fervor and in many cases kept the movement going where it had slowed down. When the picketing started, it was the girls who were most faithful about being on the line every day. These girls would be living in the South when they got out of college, had less chance of moving out than the boys, and they did not want their children to grow up in the same society they had. In Tallahassee, Florida, a mother rushed to pay bond for her daughter who was in jail, arrested in a sit-in. The girl would not let her mother pay bond: "Mamma, I love you, but I am not free, and I am not free because your generation didn't act, but I want my children to be free. That's why I'll stay in jail."

In sit-ins across the nation many white youths participated in this movement of youth and of students. But it was principally the Negro's fight, and the white students who participated saw little action. One Chicago white student who drove all the way to Raleigh for the conference on April 16 concluded, "With or without the help of Northern students, the South is changing." It was with a certain longing that this young man looked on the Negro student's fight, something he could only watch: "The young Southern Negro today is understandably having one of the best times of his life in the process of fighting for his rights. For once he is participating in a meaningful action."

But if this was a movement of Negro youth, there were also significant changes in the parents. There was a certain shame, a humiliation at first, as older Negroes saw their

158

Nearing the end: sitting in at Woolworth's, May, 1960. Photo: Greensboro Daily News.

children fighting something they had been willing to accept for many years. Louis Lomax in *The Negro Revolt* describes this humiliation:

> There is nothing more humiliating to a Negro man who cleans cuspidors and bows before white patrons in an all-white barber shop than to see a nine-year-old Negro child, head high, face well scrubbed, walk through a howling mob and flying bricks to go to school. He hates himself—God, how he hates himself. . . .

The sit-ins, however, enabled many older Negroes to take part, to do something. All Negroes could participate in the boycotts that exerted such tremendous pressure on Southern merchants, and as more demonstrations took place, more of the adult Negroes, the parents of the students, took part. One observer wrote: "The genius of the demonstrations lies in their spirituality; in their ability to enlist every Negro, from laborer to the leader, and inspire him to seek suffering as a badge of honor."

In Orangeburg, South Carolina, police turned high-powered water hoses on demonstrators and then herded them all into an open stockade. That evening a group of old Negro tenant farmers, the dirt farmers who had been a symbol of oppression in the South since the Civil War, came to the campus and went to one of the teachers. "What are you gonna do about all them chillun that got hosed?" They were there to help. In Nashville during a rush by Negro lawyers and businessmen with bail money for jailed students, a judge asked a nearby Negro attorney, "Are all the Negro lawyers of Nashville representing the defendants?" "Every one!" he was told. "That's the finest spirit of stick-togetherness I've ever seen in your community," said

160

the judge, "Me too, your honor," was the reply. The sit-ins provided a stimulus in the Negro community, and the adults rallied behind the students.

The demonstrations also had important effects on Negro leadership and organizations in the community, for they became a form of protest against the Negro establishment. Bayard Rustin wrote, "What the student movement has done is to have broken the back of professional Uncle Tomism. For years the Negro middle class has profited from segregation. . . ." And James Lawson wrote, "This movement is not only against segregation. It's against Uncle Tom Negroes, against the NAACP's over reliance on the courts, and against the futile middle-class techniques of sending letters to the centers of power."

One of the most significant changes among Negro organizations came in the NAACP. Organized in 1909, the NAACP came to almost absolute power among civil rights organizations in the late forties after a series of successful court decisions. In the fifties it continued its policy of legalism, concentrating on desegregating the schools, and few Negroes openly opposed its policies. But in 1960 only about 6 percent of Southern Negro children were in schools with whites, and the mass of Negro adults, college students, and most children had been unaffected by desegregation. This 6 percent represented a dramatic gain, but it failed to touch the masses or make them enthusiastic.

The sit-ins were something that did appeal to the masses, something in which they could participate, and the organization's leadership was challenged. The NAACP soon sent youth workers into the Southern communities to try to help the protesting students, but it was no longer leading the students; it was only following, hoping to keep up. As Louis Lomax pointed out, "The impact of these new

161

student demonstrations was such that the NAACP was forced to support the students or face a revolt by the Southern rank and file." The NAACP did try to get some credit for the sit-ins. Roy Wilkins, executive secretary of the organization, said, "NAACP college youth members were among the four who made history in the 1960s' first sit-in at Greensboro," and in its semiofficial history by Langston Hughes published in 1962, the NAACP is given credit for the idea of the sit-ins for their work in Oklahoma City in 1958. The facts are that none of the four in Greensboro had heard of the demonstrations in Oklahoma City until after February 1, 1960, and none were members of the organization at that time.

In 1961, membership in the NAACP dropped by several thousand; but more important, new civil rights groups were on the scene to take much of the glory that had belonged previously to the NAACP. CORE, formed in the forties but relatively unknown up to 1960, was doing much of the work in guiding the students. Dr. Martin Luther King Jr.'s Southern Christian Leadership Conference (SCLC) gained new momentum from these demonstrations, and the Student Nonviolent Coordinating Committee (SNICK) was a direct outgrowth of the sit-ins. In Greensboro the NAACP remained the primary civil rights organization, but Dr. George Simkins, who was head of the local group, received some criticism from the national group for reportedly calling in CORE to help the students. At the 1960 convention Greensboro was the last city to be recognized, and the NAACP minutes stated that the sit-ins were spontaneous and had begun in 1958 in Oklahoma City.

The Greensboro Negro community was pleased and proud that the sit-ins started in their city. In the first few days there was some hostility among Negroes toward the

162

movement, and Ezell Blair Sr. remembers that while his family was never bothered by whites during this period, some Negroes treated them rather coldly. The professional classes, especially the ministers and doctors, were slow to support the students, and some supported them only toward the end of the demonstrations. But for the most part, the older Negroes were for the students from the beginning and tried to help in any way possible, and for Dr. Simkins and the local NAACP it was a shot in the arm. Membership increased significantly, and no longer was there the complacency that had marked the attitude of adult Negroes. Many were moved to action. Dr. Simkins, when asked during the protest whether the sit-ins would set back school desegregation, replied: "If anything they will hasten it. They will make Negroes more conscious of their rights. It will make them feel that they should seek their rights more. The trouble with the school thing is that we haven't had applicants to file for the white schools." In the next few years, many more Greensboro Negroes applied to the "white schools."

Both individuals and the community changed, but to many the biggest change was among the faculty and administration at A & T. With the school's history, with the dependence on state funds, with its tradition of conservative presidents and faculty hired to conform, many were surprised that the administration did not come out in complete opposition to the sit-ins. Ezell Blair Sr. said he was amazed at their response. Even in the late fifties under the administration of Dr. Gibbs, Martin Luther King Jr. and Thurgood Marshall had been denied the right to speak on campus because they were too controversial, and it was generally conceded that the Gibbs administration and faculty followed in the mold of previous administrations.

But "things were changing every day and every hour

163

within the school," as Dr. Simkins put it. The sit-ins caused considerable soul-searching on the part of the academicians, and teachers came out in support of the students. School facilities were used by the students for mimeographing demonstration material, and attendance rolls were forgotten by some members of the faculty.

To the more militant Negroes, the biggest change occurred in Dr. Gibbs. He had been at the school for thirty years, was a member of the Bluford "team," and had been hand-picked by Bluford to succeed him. When he made no move to restrict the students many were surprised, feeling that Bluford would surely have stopped them. Several reasons were given for Gibbs's lack of action. One man close to the administration said, "We came to the realization that all the time he was no conservative." Another felt Gibbs did not want to lose face in the Negro community. (After the booing episode in 1955, Dr. Bluford had sent a strong apology to Governor Hodges. Many thought that Hodges should have apologized to A & T, and Bluford's esteem in the Negro community went down.) But if these reasons give some indication as to why the man acted as he did, they perhaps do not tell the whole story.

Dr. Gibbs is a kindly, gracious, and courtly gentleman with white hair. He is of the old school, and a hundred years ago one might have been inclined to call him "uncle" as a term of respect—except that the term "uncle" simply does not lend itself to a college president with two degrees from Harvard. Gibbs came to A & T in 1926 as a teacher in history and government. He later became dean of the School of Education and General Studies, and when Dr. Bluford died in 1955 he was made president. More than an administrator, Gibbs was a teacher and a scholar, and to his students he was a "great social science instructor."

164

Even after he retired from the presidency of A & T, Gibbs remained at the college to continue teaching and to work on the school's archives, a task he loved. And so, although he may have changed, he may have always been liberal, and he may have been worried about saving face, but when in 1960 the students came in to tell him about the sit-ins, Gibbs acted as the scholar. As the scholar, the academician, he went by the rules, and there was nothing in the college rules that said the students could not do something of this sort on their own free time. True, he was worried about violence, and he questioned whether the trustees or the state might not do something about the college's appropriations. But seeing no rules to cover the situation, he was not going to restrict the students because some people disliked what they were doing. He simply turned the matter over to the dean of men. If any of the boys got in trouble, they would be dealt with there.

There were no excuses made to city or state officials, or trustees. They were told exactly what was happening. Mayor Roach went to talk to Gibbs several times about the sit-ins, and was told that there were simply no regulations to cover the students. Roach felt that Gibbs was very diplomatic, but he also thought he was "wholly in favor of their demands." In March, Gibbs made his annual report to the trustees. He explained that he had had no prior knowledge of the demonstrations and had not given his consent, and he then went on to say:

> The students feel deeply and sincerely that they have important basic interests at stake in the situation. They feel these matters so strongly that threats of arrest or intimidation do not seem to deter them. Consequently, this feeling must be understood in dealing with them in order to maintain their cooperation.

. . . our students were well-behaved, respectful, and peaceful, both toward college authorities and store managers.

. . . the students have cooperated well, and all cooperating agencies are hopeful that something constructive will be worked out in the near future.

Late in February, when A & T had to make its annual appeal to the state legislature for appropriations, the administration came under fire from Representative John Kerr of Warren County, in the eastern part of the state: "Is it not a fact that your students are participating in sit-down strikes in Greensboro with respect to eating places? Yet you come down here to white people and beg for money. We're getting tired of this. . . . You can strike all you please, but don't come here and beg us." Dr. Louis G. Dowdy, who was representing A & T, did not deny the charges made by the representative and made no excuses for the college. Nonetheless, A & T received a larger appropriation from the state that year than it ever had before.

9

The Solution

For God's sake, George,
you've got to do something!

ON JULY 25, it was all over. At 2 P.M. three well-dressed Negroes sat down at the Woolworth's lunch counter and were served. There had been no advance publicity, and there was no trouble. The three were employees of Woolworth's. The afternoon paper headlined, "Lunch Counters Integrated Here," and reported that the action by both Woolworth's and Kress's had been purely voluntary.

C. L. Harris released a statement to the press: "The Mayor's Advisory Committee has recommended that all stores selling merchandise and dispensing food serve all customers. We have agreed to abide by this recommendation." Dr. Hobart Jarrett, president of the Greensboro Citizens Association, an adult-Negro group, said, "We are pleased to have had this opportunity to work cooperatively with the Mayor's Committee and the operators on this matter which is significant to our city." And Ed Zane, who had done so much in the preceding months, also released a statement: "To a commendable extent the events of today and tomorrow therefore will not be the unthinking reflection of slogans and precast concepts but will be the honest attempts of individuals to act according to the finest that is within them. Greensboro citizens can be counted on to accept with tolerance and to understand actions taken in such a spirit."

That was all there was. The next morning the *Daily News* gave the story only a one-column head on the local page, and reported that during the day only nine Negroes had asked for service at Woolworth's. There were no pictures. In the following week, the newspapers had little to report. The articles usually gave the number of Negroes served and reported whether there had been any incidents. On the twenty-seventh, three white patrons left when Negroes sat beside them, and one complained to the manager, but during that day fifty Negroes had been served with no difficulty.

In the first week, approximately three hundred Negroes were served at Woolworth's. On the twenty-eighth, the Guilford Dairy Bar served two, and shortly after that, Meyer's department store opened its lunch counter. After that first week, there was no mention of the stores in the local press, and in the city the opening of the counters to Negroes seemed to have made little impression. As the *Daily News* said in an editorial, "There was no fuss and furor. Negroes did not request service *en masse*. They came as individuals and they were served as individuals. The sky did not fall."

The break had come in early June. George Roach was welcoming ladies to the opening of the Merchants Association summer movie series, held each Wednesday at the Carolina Theatre. This was the type of duty Mayor Roach welcomed, and he was enjoying himself. After he had given a speech to the women and shaken some hands, the movie began and he left. Coming out of the theatre, he was met by C. L. Harris: "For God's sake, George, you've got to do something!"

168

Mayor Roach reminded Harris that he had the Mayor's Committee to deal with the situation and suggested he go see Ed Zane. But Harris's relations with Zane had been strained at times, and instead he went to see another committee member, Arnold Schiffman. Now discussions were begun on opening the counters.

Harris had known long before June that he was going to integrate. In early May the regional office had told him, "Integrate when the time is right." The decision as to just when that might be was left largely up to Harris, and he has said it was completely his own decision; but there must have been some pressure on him to act. In Winston-Salem when the Woolworth's counters integrated on May 25, the store manager, who had been with the company for thirty-seven years, retired. He announced: "Before I will desegregate my lunch counters and subject my many thousands of customers and friends to something they do not want I will retire from the company." Harris did not want to integrate while there was still outside pressure on him, and he waited until the college was out. High school students still picketed, trained by the college students, but the mass of students who had earlier tried to force him to act were no longer present.

After Harris went to Arnold Schiffman, the Mayor's Committee acted only in an advisory capacity. They helped arrange meetings between the store owners (Kress's and Woolworth's) and such groups as the Greensboro Citizens Association, the Negro men's group, and individuals like Dean Gamble. The initiative was largely Harris's, and he set the conditions. He "reserved the right to discriminate against those not clothed well," and he was not about to let the committee know what day he was going to integrate. He wanted no advance publicity, and the press agreed not

169

to take pictures. Most important, Harris wanted to keep the situation in his own hands, and he wanted the first Negroes served to be his employees.

The Greensboro Citizens Association was composed of the presidents or chairmen of all the Negro organizations in Greensboro. It had taken no part in the first weeks of the demonstrations. Individual members such as Dr. George Simkins and Reverend Otis Hairston were involved, but it was only later, when the variety stores wanted some responsible adult group with which to negotiate, that the association became active. There was some criticism of members for coming in at the last for the glory, but the president of the group, Dr. Hobart Jarrett, a professor at Bennett College, had been one of the leaders in trying to organize negotiations. When they were organized, one observer remembers, Jarrett was "instrumental in keeping negotiations on a high plane." The group realized it had no control over the students, but there was no apparent antagonism between the older and younger groups, and the adults agreed that the students would have to pass on anything decided upon in negotiations between the association and the variety stores.

When the conditions were finally agreed upon in July, the word had to be spread throughout the Negro community; this was done largely by the churches. Ministers announced during the services that the stores were integrating, but they requested that their parishioners refrain from converging on the stores all at once.

One of the big fears of the store owners had been that they would be inundated with Negroes. It was agreed, therefore, that no Negroes would come between 11:30 A.M. and 2 P.M., the busiest times at the local stores, during the first week. Other control measures as to the number of

170

Negroes that would come were decided upon, but after the first few days Harris called up the Citizens Association and other groups involved in the integration of the stores and told them he didn't care if it was controlled or not. Things had been going smoothly, and he simply didn't want to be bothered.

Harris still wanted other stores besides Kress's to go along with him, and during these last weeks Ed Zane and his committee had been holding meetings with them to try and work something out. But by the end of July only two other stores, the Guilford Dairy Bar and Meyer's luncheonette, were willing to integrate. The Citizens Association was high in its praise of the Guilford Dairy Bar and its manager, Mose Kiser. There had been little pressure to open the dairy bars, except for occasional picketing at a few shopping centers. But Kiser came of his own accord to discuss the integration of his counters, and shortly afterward he also began a program of hiring Negroes to work behind the counter.

However, as before, most of the other stores felt it was not their problem. Some were willing to desegregate if the rest went along, but none wanted to pioneer. Ed Zane received a letter that showed how the manager of one store felt:

> As I told you on yesterday, we want to try to reach some kind of understanding about this problem, but [this store] is not interested in taking a heroic stand in this instance. We are willing to cooperate in some way that will be mutually beneficial to all concerned. I again want to emphasize that we do not want to see an agreement whereby we and the variety stores are located in a type of ghetto, and I am hopeful you will be able to get a large number

171

of the stool or counter operated lunch rooms to agree to this program.

For that matter, Woolworth's did not want to take a "heroic stand" either. The reluctance of merchants to change and the slowness with which they acted was well explained early in April when the Southern Regional Council released a revised account of *The Student Protest Movement, Winter 1960:*

> That . . . cities have not yet succeeded in resolving the dilemma is not surprising when it is recognized that the initial call for leadership was directed at merchants, a group sensitive to so many pressures as to be peculiarly unprepared for the role of leading social change. Unless [the merchants] . . . can be supported, and, in fact, led by persons or groups of acknowledged prestige, it is fruitless to expect merchants to decide what shall be the social practices of the community.

That the variety stores did not want this "role of leading social change" was made quite clear from Harris's insistence on "local custom" all the way up to the president of F. W. Woolworth. At the annual meeting of Woolworth's stockholders, held on May 18 in Watertown, New York, and picketed by twenty-two people, Robert C. Kirkwood, president of the company, made a statement of the company's view of the demonstrations. He told stockholders that Woolworth's would continue a policy of adhering to "local custom established by local people for the conduct of business in the community," and he pointed out that 87 percent of Woolworth's lunch counters around the country were integrated. Then he said, "Dealing as we are with the deep-rooted convictions of the people of the South, it is hardly realistic to suppose that any company is influential enough to suddenly change its thinking on this subject." P. H. Werner of the Atlanta office, in a statement made in Greensboro, also pointed out the reluctance of the company to do anything without the support of other businessmen. "When these demonstrations started, we felt that as a company with headquarters outside the state we didn't want to start any integration without the cooperation of other retail businessmen. . . . We proposed that we would go along on a planned integration program in cooperation with other merchants."

But Woolworth's and Kress's did integrate without the "cooperation of other retail businessmen," and in opposition to "the deep-rooted convictions of the people of the South," and without regard for "local custom." They integrated when only two of the twelve downtown eating establishments were willing to go along. What changed the variety stores' attitude on this, and what finally solved the lunch-counter crisis?

In discussing the sit-ins, the people involved have expressed many different opinions. The motivation of the four boys, the bomb scare, the role of the press, the influence of the Mayor's Committee, and Greensboro's leadership—all have evoked varied responses. But to the question of what drove the variety stores to serve Negroes at their counters, the answer has always been the same. C. L. Harris, Ralph Johns, Ed Zane, Dr. George Simkins, and George Roach all agree: it was the tremendous economic pressure put on the stores by the Negroes' boycott, along with the reticence of whites to trade there because of fear of trouble.

For the downtown Woolworth's, 1959 had been the best year the store had ever had. It was fourth in the Atlanta district in food sales and eighth in district merchandise sales. Then came 1960. The first week of the sit-ins, sales were down $6,000. The second week they were down $6,700. Sales picked up slightly after that week, but after the failure of negotiations the Negroes started the full-scale boycott. In January 1960, Woolworth's had made a survey of local store sales. According to Harris, the survey had been taken to determine whether a Negro lunch counter was needed, and in a speech made in May to the Lion's Club, he said the survey revealed that Negro trade accounted for only 4.78 percent of the total sales—a total that did not include the white lunch counter. But the loss of that 4.78 percent and the loss of people who simply stopped trading at Woolworth's nearly wiped out the profits for 1960. That year alone cost the store $200,000 in sales, and it dropped to eighth in food sales and tenth in merchandise in the district.

Moral considerations and the rights of the Negro, then, had little to do with Woolworth's decision to desegregate. They were mentioned often enough, but when it came to a solution money was the deciding factor. There were those who did act for moral reasons. Ed Zane is one. He honestly felt segregation was wrong, and he felt an obligation to do something. He later realized that the sit-ins were successful for economic reasons, and although he was extremely relieved that a solution was found, he regretted that in today's world moral considerations, integrity, and convictions count for so little. "You can take a man with all the integrity in the world, but if you offer him enough money, he will probably have his price." Ed Zane did not have a price.

Ralph Johns is another who acted for moral reasons, but Ralph Johns had two hundred thousand dollars' worth of uncollected debts pasted on his walls, and to at least one

174

of the four boys who started the sit-ins, Ralph Johns was a "fool." "You can't operate a business that way," the student said. It is true that Ralph Johns with his debts, his lack of good, hard business sense, his low regard in the community, had little influence and could make few people move. But to hear him called a fool by one of the few people that he did have an influence on, that he did get to move, is strange. Somehow a different evaluation of the man is expected.

C. L. Harris was another who recognized the moral aspects of the situation. To the Woolworth's manager little was more important than business and economics, but privately he admitted, "Morally we were wrong, sure. But so was the entire community." And although Harris may have been making excuses for Woolworth's, he was also right. He pointed to the 72 percent of the people who wrote in to the Mayor's Committee saying they favored integration of the counters; most of these people never ate at Woolworth's, and they could afford to be big about a little ten cent store.

When the business leaders talked about a solution, it was always, "We don't want another Montgomery," or "We don't want another Little Rock"; these men were afraid of what something like that might do to business and prospective industry. And when local citizens talked about a solution, it was usually because they didn't want to see their home town spread across the nation's newspapers as a city of hate and violence. They were proud of Greensboro, they had generally grown up with the town, and they wanted to see the city continue to grow.

These were not moral considerations. But for an America in 1960 which had seen the payola scandals, which had seen Charles Van Doren admit he received answers on a quiz show, which had seen the President of the United States deny knowledge of any U-2 planes—to act because you were proud of your city, because you had a stake in its future growth, because you happened to like your job and wanted to do what was best for the company —these did not seem like such bad reasons to many people.

In September, when the students returned, many went down to Woolworth's and Kress's to eat. Some went to test it out, but for many it was no longer a novelty, for in that summer of 1960 thirty-two other Southern cities desegregated some of their eating facilities. By June of 1961, 126 cities in the South had some integrated facilities. It had all started in Greensboro, and although Greensboro had taken six months, the lunch-counter problem was solved. Some Southern cities took less time; others more. But these cities, including Greensboro, were to discover that the problem was not limited to public lunch counters. Change, the entire country was to find, had just begun.

Epilogue

GREENSBORO has changed in the decade of the sixties. The feeling of growth of 1960 has become reality, and with it have come many of the problems common to larger cities. Greensboro today is a spread-out, almost sprawling city with new developments, new industries, and new residents. It is still growing, still conscious of its image, and perhaps overly conscious of what other Southern cities, particularly Atlanta and Charlotte, are doing. In race relations, the non-violence of the sit-ins has changed. As in the rest of the country, new problems have come from this.

In 1963 the city had another outbreak of demonstrations with the students of A & T again playing the major role. Led by student body president Jesse Jackson (who was also a part-time employee of Ralph Johns), the protests were directed against the restaurants, movie theatres, motels, and other places of public accommodation whose owners in 1960 had considered the problem limited to the variety stores. And in these demonstrations, it was not only college students who participated. Parents, grandparents, children, high school students, and some adult white sympathizers all staged non-violent mass marches on downtown Greensboro in an effort to break down these barriers of segregation. They courted arrest and were arrested—approximately 432 in one night, and over a thousand during the demonstrations. Once again the white community formed a Mayor's Committee, and once again, after extended negotiations, these places were opened to Negroes.

In 1968 the death of Martin Luther King, Jr. sparked more demonstrations, but these were not non-violent. When the demonstrators started smashing windows, the National Guard was immediately called out. The next day there were shotgun blasts and gunfire in east Greensboro. A & T was recessed early for Easter, and a 7:00 curfew was imposed in the city.

But the 1968 violence was mild compared to that which arose over a seemingly insignificant incident at Dudley High School. At the still all-Negro school, a student was not allowed to run for president of the student body— because, he said, he was a member of the Youth for Unity of a Black Society. The school administration said it was because of his grades. Whatever the reason, there were violent demonstrations at Dudley. The police were called in, and when they used tear gas to disperse the crowds, A & T students came to the support of Dudley. When it was all over, one A & T student had been killed, four policemen wounded, the National Guard called out, and A & T turned into what resembled an armed camp. One white truck driver had been pulled from his vehicle, taken inside a dorm, and beaten while his truck was burned outside. Once again a curfew was imposed, and once again A & T was let out early so that students would be off campus.

For most people in Greensboro, the 1960 sit-ins are only a vague memory if they are remembered at all. Many people confuse them with the 1963 demonstrations, and can only recall that Greensboro was "first" in having a

178

sit-in. But those who do remember are the ones directly involved, and they are quite aware of the sit-ins' significance.

C. L. Harris is retired from Woolworth's now, and if he is asked about his reaction to the events of 1960 he will say, "It was the worst happening in my life." When pressed to explain, he instead goes into sales figures, explaining that sales went down 20 percent in 1960 and that profits in the local store were off about 50 percent. He keeps talking about the sales figures, and the decline, saying it was not until 1965 that the store reached its 1959 sales level. He says that those who sat in "didn't realize what it would do to others," and then he talks about how Woolworth's has given opportunity to those who wouldn't ordinarily have had it. Woolworth's gave Harris his own opportunity, and he worked long and hard for the company, and he feels a definite loyalty. In discussing the company even now, he will say "we" had a certain sales figure for that year or "we" serve more food than the U.S. Army, and the "we" refers to Woolworth's. He doesn't need to protect Woolworth's or espouse the company line, for he is living in comfortable retirement; he simply feels that Woolworth's is the finest company in America.

And so when Harris says the sit-ins were the worst thing "he" ever went through, he really seems to mean "we," and he has feelings of resentment. It is not resentment toward the Negro, for Harris is a man who will express little open prejudice—Negroes were his customers—and he says he doesn't think integration would have come any other way except through direct action by the Negro. Nor is it resentment for what he went through personally in those six months. Rather, it is resentment for what the sit-ins did to Woolworth's. For thirty-seven years he had worked to raise the prestige of the company, to make it something more than a "five and ten," and then in one month much of this, he feels, was destroyed. Across the nation headlines blazed about the sit-ins at "five and tens" and arrests at "dime stores," and the image—not of a store that sold television sets, radios, expensive watches, and quality clothes but of a dime store refusing a customer a nickel cup of coffee—was spread across the country. This image hurt his pride, hurt him, because something he had worked for all his life was being distorted. Today he says that he would have quit the company before going through something like that again, but Harris did not quit during the sit-ins, did not ask to be transferred, and his policy of no arrests and negotiations was followed by other Woolworth stores throughout the South.

Ed Zane has aged well. He looks younger than his sixty-five-plus years, and although he has retired from Burlington Industries, he does have an office in downtown Greensboro from which he conducts his C.P.A. business. He is proud of the part he played in the 1960 sit-ins, and when he is asked about the performance of the Mayor's Committee, he will say the crisis could not have been solved without it. And then he will frankly say, "A committee is as strong as its leader," and, "I am grateful I had the capacity to work it out." He wonders how he was able to manage his own affairs while he was involved in the sit-ins, for the work of the Committee was practically a full-time job. Like Harris, Ed Zane also says he would never go through it again, but his friends feel that if the city needed his leadership through another crisis, he would undoubtedly be there.

The decade has produced ups and downs for George Dorsett. The Klan in the middle sixties enjoyed an amazing growth, and Dorsett was working full time with an expense account. But the Klan's organizational structure wasn't ready for this membership, and there was considerable internal turmoil as the Klan split into factions. Dorsett himself was banished from the United Klans of America, and the reason is not certain. The Klan says he violated a section of their by-laws on releasing news to the public (Dorsett believes any publicity is good publicity), but this seems a minor offense. It may be that he was getting too powerful, or too violent, or there may simply have been a personality difference. Dorsett then set up the Confederate Klans of America, in which he became the acting Grand Dragon, but most of his energies were expended in court. During this time he underwent a period of harassment as charges of disturbing the peace, improper mufflers, and traffic violations were brought against him. His paint-contracting business lost jobs, but he remained active in the Klan.

He is now looking to a future in which he sees the Klans reuniting. As late as three years ago, Dorsett could see the Klans gaining influence by entering candidates in political elections and testing laws through court cases. At that time he was also opposed to violence. Now he says that all avenues are closed to the Klan and that it must go completely underground. More important, he has observed the violence employed by many activist groups and feels the Klan must do likewise. "We may have to register dynamite, but there are plenty of matches in this world." He is positive there will be a revolution, and at present he sees mob rule as the only answer. He talks about the guns and weapons in his organization, and he thinks the Klan will be ready.

181

The years have not been good to Ralph Johns. Physically, he is still a strong man. His hearing is worse, and he wears bifocals, but he still retains much of the good looks of his movie days. But Ralph Johns lives alone today in a rented room. His two daughters do not speak to him, and his wife has left him. She asked him to stop his civil rights work, but he couldn't. And in 1963, when he was working with the demonstrators, she decided she'd had enough. Johns says a priest advised him to leave home for a few days until things cooled down, but when he went back three days later his wife had him moved out. He does not really blame her. There were the threats, phone calls, obscene remarks, and ostracism by her friends. The two girls had to bear the cruelty of their classmates, and it all was just too much for his family.

Johns no longer has his store, either. In 1963 he moved to South Elm Street, a half-block from Woolworth's, hoping to improve his business, but his business only became worse. He owed money to his suppliers and creditors and was unable to get fresh stock. An important factor in the store's decline was the loss of much of Johns's Negro trade. Many of the students he knew had left, and the younger Negroes no longer wanted to trade in a store that catered mainly to Negroes. They preferred the white stores where they were very welcome by the mid-sixties.

But Johns kept hanging on until 1966, when an idea—another cause—involved him. He would start a Viet Nam prisoner exchange, offering himself for any American who was held prisoner by the North Vietnamese. The story hit the wire services, and Johns had over twelve hundred volunteers to go along. He sold his store and started working full time on the project. As an exchange prisoner, he would work in hospitals or on farms or at any unrelated war ac-

Ralph Johns in the 1980s with former employee Jesse Jackson. *Photo: Greensboro News Record.*

tivity in Viet Nam. He went to Washington to try to push his idea through, but the state department gave him a polite brushoff. Once again Ralph Johns had failed.

During this period he was receiving correspondence from many people around the country, and in particular from one woman in Tennessee. When she invited him to spend New Year's with her family in Tennessee, he accepted. They became engaged shortly thereafter, and he went to Memphis to work in a clothing store. The job didn't work out—Johns couldn't get used to working for someone else. He quit and came back to Greensboro. Sympathetic manufacturers with whom he had dealt for twenty-five years supplied him with merchandise, and he opened up another store and married the woman from Tennessee. Neither the store nor the marriage worked out. She wasn't what she pretended to be, Johns says, and the store simply couldn't make it.

In 1969 things looked up for a time: the Economic Opportunity Council hired Johns as a community developer at large. Johns could not "work within the framework" (he wanted to picket food stores over prices), and after five months he was fired. He is still in Greensboro, working as the general manager of a small black newspaper, but how long he will remain, how long he can operate in *this* framework, is not certain.

Although Johns is still very active in the black Greensboro community, he does little NAACP work now, and he is, at times, bitter. He sees all the publicity and honors many of the civil rights leaders are getting, and he feels that some of this should be coming to him. He dislikes what he calls "johnny-come-latelies" who jump on the civil rights bandwagon to gain publicity. Johns will, on occasion, play

184

the martyr, and he looks into the past a great deal. He has written an autobiography, and there are two sentences in it that seem to show much of what he is thinking. "Someday I hope to come back to Chame [Panama] and see if after about thirty years if Sergeant Rafael is remembered and loved as he was in 1942," and "If I had stayed with insurance, I would be worth a million now." He is a man looking for the love he has given out but never quite received in return, and a man looking at the past, wondering what would have happened if he hadn't given and gambled his money away. For Ralph Johns, a man with no family, a man forgotten by the community, a man growing old, the past will probably always seem brighter than the future.

Most of the others involved in the 1960 sit-ins are still in Greensboro. George Roach did not run again for mayor in 1962 and is devoting full time to his realty business. He feels his stand during the sit-ins did not hurt him. Dr. George Simkins is still president of the local NAACP and very active in its affairs. Paul Calhoun is still police chief, but the 1969 violence has not made his job any easier. For the first time, charges of police brutality were made, and when the local newspapers spread these charges across their pages, there were calls for the police chief's dismissal. Today Calhoun is very guarded in answering questions, and he gives few opinions. However, he does say he feels the main result of the 1969 violence for the police department has been the difficulty in getting new men for the force, particularly Negroes.

The four boys who started it all have gone their separate ways. Joe McNeil graduated in 1963 with a degree in engineering physics, and as a member of the Air Force ROTC went directly into the service. He served six years

185

as a navigator on B-52 jets, was discharged with the rank of major, and is now with IBM in New York. Ezell Blair Jr. also graduated in 1963, and with a degree in sociology went directly to the Howard University school of law. He dropped out after a year and worked for the Job Corps in New Bedford, Massachusetts. He is now a history teacher at the Opportunity Industrialization Center in Roxbury, Massachusetts, and is married and has two daughters. He says of his present situation: "I'm not so much of a community activist as I used to be. I try to help people live a better life." Franklin McCain did not graduate until 1964; the pressures of 1960 were so great that he dropped out for a year. He lived for a time with David Richmond's parents and is now married and living in Charlotte, North Carolina, where he works for the Celanese Corporation. Of the four, only David Richmond still lives in Greensboro, and when he is asked what effect the sit-ins had on him, he will say simply that he did not graduate. He worked for a time at two jobs to earn enough so he could return to school, and he did return, but he has not yet finished.

A & T is proud of the 1960 sit-ins, but even more proud of its growth and gains in the past years. In 1967 the name was changed to A & T State University, and the administration points to the gains in the quality of student. The college board requirements have risen dramatically, as has the percentage of faculty who have their doctorates. The alumni are loyal, and Elis Corbett, now associate director of planning and development, points out that for some reason many of the more generous donors to the alumni fund are those students who took an active part in the 1960 sit-ins. The 1969 disturbance on campus was a shock to the administration and had some effect. Applications to the university went down, alumni gifts dropped over 20 percent, and some believe that certain A & T building projects planned for the school were dropped for this reason. But there is a feeling at A & T that the difficulties are over, that the school's growth will not further be hampered, and that there will be no more violence. They are not certain, but then their uncertainty, their hopes and feelings are not unique.

The Four at the 30th anniversary breakfast in Greensboro, February 1, 1990. Left to right: Joseph McNeil, Jibreel Khazan (Ezell Blair, Jr.), Franklin McCain, and David Richmond. *Photo:* Chuck Liddy, *Durham Morning Herald.*

Epilogue, 1990:
The Ordinary Men

ON FEBRUARY 1, 1990, four middle-aged men sat down at the Woolworth's lunch counter in Greensboro and had breakfast. Thirty years before, the same four had been students at A & T and were refused service, but this day was to be much different. No reporter had been present to cover that first sit-in. In 1990 the four were surrounded by reporters and onlookers. The problem with service in 1990 was caused by the crush of media and the distraction of reporters' questions. The 7:30 a.m. meal was telecast live locally and nationally.

In 1960, when they left Woolworth's, a lone photographer from the *Greensboro Record* took a picture of the four walking down Sycamore Street. In 1990, as they departed, a hundred or more TV, radio, and newspaper reporters crowded around a podium set up in front of the same Woolworth's. Cameras clicked and video cameras whirred as the four unveiled their bronze footprints implanted in the sidewalk in front of the store. As one Greensboro reporter wrote, "Not since the 1974 NCAA Final Four have so many reporters and photographers showed up in the city for an event."

In 1960 the question at City Hall was whether the students should be arrested. In 1990 the city of Greensboro helped sponsor the activities. The location of Woolworth's, at Elm and Sycamore Streets, was officially renamed "February First Place" by the city. New street signs were unveiled during the morning ceremonies.

In 1960 C. L. Harris had wanted no publicity and was left on his own to handle the problem. In 1990 Woolworth's public relations executives from New York were sent to help orchestrate the event. Both inside and outside the store, the executives, one black and one white, made certain everything ran smoothly for the hundreds who had come to witness the events.

Greensboro had changed in the thirty years since the sit-ins, and the Woolworth's store was one of the few retail establishments still in existence at the same location. Three new downtown high-rise office buildings had gone up in the 1980s, but the retail stores had long since departed for suburban malls. Woolworth's lunch counter remained one of the few places to eat in downtown Greensboro.

In the 1970s Greensboro experienced more racial unrest, but on November 3, 1979, the city saw the worst violence in its history. That Saturday, a march was planned by the Communist Workers party (CWP) through Morningside Heights, a black neighborhood. The march was called "Death to the Klan," and the CWP and black and white radicals told the police to stay away. They had dared the Klan and American Nazi groups to show up. These groups did show up, and when the shooting stopped, five members of the Communist Workers party were dead. Although both groups were composed primarily of non-Greensboro residents, the shootings shook Greensboro's image as a place where racial problems could be worked out peacefully. In three separate trials, no one was ever convicted in the killings, and the sit-ins' example of non-violence seemed far away.

The significance of the Greensboro sit-ins grew over the years, both locally and nationally, and anniversary celebrations were held in both 1980 and 1985. The thirtieth anniversary, however, was much larger than the first two. All the institutions that were involved in 1960—the city of Greensboro, Woolworth's, and A & T State University—welcomed the attention, and three days of events were held. Even the original lunch-counter stools were presented by Woolworth's to the Greensboro Historical Museum to be placed on permanent display.

A & T took particular pride in the event and used it to show off its growing status to both its own students and to the world. Two of the children of the Greensboro Four (as the four who first sat-in were now called) were students at A & T. They were part of the planning committee for the ceremonies. A sculpted bronze frieze of the Greensboro Four was unveiled on campus, and lectures and symposiums were held by the university throughout the celebration.

A surprising number of those involved in the 1960 sit-ins were around thirty years later. Two waitresses who had been working at the lunch counter the day the four were refused service still worked at the lunch counter. At the anniversary breakfast, they served the four. C. L. Harris, now eighty-five, was not part of the ceremonies. Although he had been retired from Woolworth's for twenty years, he still worried about the store's image. "Don't call it a dime store," he told a reporter calling for an interview. "We were once a dime store but not since 1934." He had binders filled with clippings of the sit-ins, but he did not

191

have good memories. "It was a sad experience. . . . I am ready to forget it."

The Rev. George Dorsett was certainly not part of the ceremonies and was no longer listed in the Greensboro phone directory. On December 10, 1975, a Senate Intelligence Committee source had revealed that Dorsett was a paid FBI informant. In an FBI memorandum entitled "Disruption of Hate Groups," Dorsett was described as having worked for the FBI since 1967 when he had broken from the United Klan and had formed the rival Confederate Klan. The FBI had helped him organize the new Klan. In a meeting of the Klan on January 12, 1976, Dorsett was formally banished forever from that organization.

Ed Zane, at ninety-one, remained active and alert. He was still a business consultant in town and occasionally ate at Woolworth's. He took part in some of the activities of the thirtieth anniversary. He remained concerned about racial problems and wondered about the emphasis the black leaders placed on A & T remaining a predominantly black institution. To him such efforts seemed inconsistent with the struggle for integration. "That just doesn't make sense to me," he said.

Ralph Johns had left Greensboro in the early 1970s, but he returned to visit in February 1990 and be part of the celebration. He was not greatly changed. At age seventy-three he was grayer, but there was a prosperous, distinguished look about him which had not been part of his last years in Greensboro. With the mass of media present, Ralph was charged with the old energy. It may have been the Greensboro Four's day, but Ralph hoped his involvement in the start of the sit-ins would be noticed and that he would be recognized. He told reporters who would listen of his civil rights struggles. He recounted the stories of his

192

battles with the Klan, the death threats, and his estrangement from his children. He showed the photographs of his career in an album he kept in his coat pocket, and now there were additional shots of Ralph with Mike Tyson, Kenny Rogers, Ricardo Montalban, and other celebrities.

When Ralph left Greensboro he had gone to California, taking a job with the *Beverly Hills Courier,* a weekly newspaper. When he retired in 1989 he was associate publisher and national account executive. For the former World's Greatest Gate Crasher and Hollywood extra, Southern California was appropriate territory. His paper covered much of the entertainment business, and he was able to rub elbows with Hollywood celebrities. His new scrapbook was testimony to that. He remarried in the mid-1980s, and his wife Norma seemed at times taken aback by his energy and ideas. He currently was trying to integrate an Elks Club in Orange County, California, and she smiled as she said the Elks didn't know what had hit them since Ralph joined the club.

A national wire service story on Ralph in 1989 had indicated he was bitter over his lack of recognition: "I just want somebody to say, 'Hey Ralph, thanks a hell of a lot for what you've done.'" He felt that recent works on the sit-ins had downplayed or even ignored his role, and he believed the reason might be because he was white. But some remembered. Dr. George Simkins, still practicing dentistry in the city, did not hesitate to give Ralph credit. "He *was* the sit-in. There's no question about it, it was his idea." And in Greensboro, as he stood in front of Woolworth's that first day of February thirty years later, scores of older black friends came up and hugged him and shook his hand. He beamed. He was not totally forgotten.

Dr. Warmoth T. Gibbs was ninety-five, but he still

193

made it to some of the ceremonies. He was a revered figure at A & T. He drew a standing ovation at a luncheon during the celebration, and Franklin McCain introduced him, in a speech, as "my main man."

The four freshmen, now middle-aged men approaching fifty, all were present for the ceremonies. They had come from quiet walks of life to be the center of attention for the day. Joseph McNeil, with six years in the air force after A & T, remained active in the reserves and was a colonel. He now lived in New York state where he was an administrator with the Federal Aviation Agency. He had also been a stockbroker in Fayetteville, North Carolina, and a commercial banker in New York City.

Franklin McCain's years after A & T were spent in Charlotte, North Carolina, as an executive for the Celanese Corporation. The father of three, McCain met regularly with Charlotte teenagers to encourage them to stay in school. While he never ran for public office, he was active in local politics, and one black Charlotte politician lauded him by saying, "He is still in the business of making change."

Ezell Blair, Jr., might have shown the most apparent change of the four in the years since A & T. In 1970 he took the Islamic name Jibreel Khazan, and at the anniversary celebration he wore flowing robes with his long hair and beard. He still made his home in New Bedford, Massachusetts, with his wife and three children. He worked in several jobs over the years, but currently he was teaching those with developmental disabilities. In an interview a few weeks before the anniversary, he refused to talk about society's problems in terms of black and white: "As long as we stay in the color game, we will never be free as individuals."

194

Of the four men, David Richmond had experienced the roughest road. He had never finished work for his degree at A & T, though most of his years after leaving school had been spent in Greensboro. He was now divorced. He went through several jobs and for a while moved to the mountains of North Carolina where he lived as a near recluse. But he returned in 1981 to care for his ailing parents. Both had died in the eighteen months preceding the thirtieth anniversary, and he still felt their loss deeply. Two weeks before the celebration he was fired from his job at a nursing home where he had worked for nine years. Richmond, now bearded and balding, remained a quiet, shy individual who wondered if his involvement in the sit-ins might have made it tough for him to find a job in Greensboro. "Everyone thought of me as a threat, and I'm the most passive person you ever met."

At a luncheon on the campus of A & T on February 1, Harvey Gantt, former black mayor of Charlotte, was the featured speaker. The day before, he had announced he would run for the U.S. Senate against the incumbent Jesse Helms. He praised the four, as all speakers had done that day. He recounted how he had been a high school student in Charleston, South Carolina, when the sit-ins first happened. He remembered how he was inspired to do something, and because there was no black college in Charleston, he became part of the group of Charleston high school students who led the sit-ins in that city. But for all the proclamations, the plaques, the footprints, the friezes, and the speeches, Harvey Gantt seemed to hit closest to the meaning of the events that were happening in Greensboro when he said, "This is the celebration of ordinary men who did extraordinary things."

When it was finally time for the four to rise and speak,

they appeared to be four unassuming men who were unimpressed with their canonization that day, each with a level perspective despite all the praise heaped on them. They spoke quietly, and in contrast to the scores of other speakers took only a few minutes at the microphone.

Joseph McNeil was the first to stand up. "I like to think of the Greensboro Four as symbols," he said, "as symbols of all students—in Tiananmen Square or in Johannesburg. We are also symbols of community, of people working together for change." His hair was the grayest of the four, and he looked the part of the banker he had once been. "We are ordinary people who did not use the sit-ins as a vehicle to promote ourselves."

It was then David Richmond's turn. "Heroes we are not. So many people shaped us. We pay homage to you. Do not celebrate us as heroes. You are the heroes. We are the product of the influence of many others. You know who you are. God bless you."

Jibreel Khazan (Ezell Blair, Jr.) came to the microphone. Even with a robe and turban and full beard, the bouncy, free-spirited freshman of thirty years before came out. He offered a prayer to the life giver, and he thanked God for his three friends and his parents. "Our parents made the sacrifices. We stand on the shoulders of all the people in Greensboro who made this possible." He spoke a little longer than the first two, and then, looking out into the crowd, he recognized Ralph Johns and asked him to stand. "Many people thought Ralph was crazy, but he wasn't. Ralph, I love you."

Franklin McCain was the last to get up and speak. He had put on weight over the years, but his face seemed the closest of the four to the freshman of thirty years before. "I accept your awards with humility and with hope, too.

By honoring us, you honor yourselves." And then he turned to the crowd. "As I grow older, I find that the people I respected in my youth, I respect even more today." He then asked Ed Zane to stand. "You were one man a seventeen-year-old could respect and trust." He then spoke to ninety-five-year-old Dr. Warmoth T. Gibbs: "You taught us what integrity was all about. From the bottom of our hearts we thank you."

And because he was the last, Franklin McCain seemed to want to make certain he had not forgotten anyone in the crowd. He looked around, smiled, and said he would like to introduce his family. As soon as he said this, the other three quickly got up and rushed to the podium. The day had been serious, and the speeches serious. But now all four were grinning and wanting to say something. They did not want to forget to introduce their own families.

It was the ordinary men speaking. As family men they were prouder of their sons and daughters than of any personal deeds. And as the wives stood and their nearly grown kids, all slightly embarrassed, stood, the faces of the Greensboro Four lit up more than at any time during the adulation that had been heard throughout the day. Their legacy to the world was the start of a movement, and they knew, as Joseph McNeil had said, they were symbols for that movement. But like ordinary men, good men, the legacy they took most pride in was their families. After the ceremonies were over they would go back to their families and continue with their lives. But unlike most ordinary men, they knew that at one time they had done something extraordinary. By taking a seat, they had changed the course of a society.

A marker erected in Greensboro in 1980 by the state of North Carolina. *Photo: Greensboro News Record.*

Index

199

200

201

Marshall, Thurgood, 126, 154, 163
Maxton (N.C.), 133
Maybank, Burnett, 119
Mayor's Committee on Community
  Relations, 87, 92, 94, 109–113,
  121, 125, 126, 137, 167, 169,
  173, 175, 180
McCain, Franklin, 15, 16, 24, 27,
  37, 95, 96, 98, 100, 101, 105,
  186, 194, 196–197
McNeil, Joseph, 15, 16, 24, 26–27,
  37, 57, 95, 96, 101, 105, 139,
  155, 185, 196, 197
Memphis, 116, 184
Merchants Association, 87, 137, 168
Meyer's department store, 168, 171
Miami, 116
Mobile (Ala.), 28, 64
Moebes, Jack, 18
Montalban, Ricardo, 193
Montgomery (Ala.), 63, 117, 119
Montgomery *Advertiser*, 119
Montgomery bus boycott, 66, 101,
  102, 157
Moore, Douglas, 83
Morehouse College, 69
Morningside Heights, 190
Morrill Act, 70

Nashville, 63, 117, 120, 136, 149,
  160
Nashville *Banner*, 120
National Association for the
  Advancement of Colored People
  (NAACP), 17, 25, 29, 35, 36,
  39, 83, 115, 140, 147, 154,
  161–163, 184, 185
National Guard, 178
National Student Association, 64
Nazi groups, 190
Negro colleges in South, 59, 68–69

Negro Revolt, 160
New Bedford (Mass.), 186
New Haven, 63
New York City, 63, 64
New York Times, 58, 76
Nixon, Richard, 57, 117
Norfolk, 142
Norfolk *Journal and Guide*, 115,
  142
North Carolina A & T, 11, 16,
  18–19, 25, 29, 31, 33, 37, 41,
  47, 50, 53, 57, 58, 59, 67, 68,
  69, 70, 84, 93, 95, 107, 109,
  113, 138, 149, 157, 163–166,
  178, 186–187, 191, 192
North Carolina Association of
  Quality Restaurants, 46
North Carolina College, 61, 63, 83
North Carolina Defenders of States
  Rights, 80
North Carolina State University, 70

Oklahoma City, 12, 162
Orangeburg (S.C.), 63, 119, 160

Pace Institute, 88
Page, Geraldine, 63
Parents, changing attitudes of,
  158–161
Patterson, Frederick D., 80, 151
Patterson, John, 63
Petersburg (Va.), 116
Phelps-Stokes Fund, 80, 151
Picketing, 107, 108, 128, 136, 147
Pilot Life Insurance Co., 75
Pittsburgh *Post Gazette*, 20
Player, Willa, 48
Police behavior, 141–145
Pope, Liston, 120
Portsmouth (Va.), 62
Price, David, 37

202

203